Reading at War
1939–45

Reading at War
1939–45

David Bilton

PEN & SWORD
HISTORY

AN IMPRINT OF PEN & SWORD BOOKS LTD.
YORKSHIRE – PHILADELPHIA

First published in Great Britain in 2020 by
Pen & Sword Military
An imprint of
Pen & Sword Books Ltd
Yorkshire – Philadelphia

ISBN 978 1 47389 1 012

A CIP catalogue record for this book is
available from the British Library.

Printed and bound in England by TJ International, Padstow, Cornwall

Pen & Sword Books Limited incorporates the imprints of Atlas,
Archaeology, Aviation, Discovery, Family History, Fiction, History,
Maritime, Military, Military Classics, Politics, Select, Transport,
True Crime, Air World, Frontline Publishing, Leo Cooper,
Remember When, Seaforth Publishing, The Praetorian Press,
Wharncliffe Local History, Wharncliffe Transport,
Wharncliffe True Crime and White Owl.

For a complete list of Pen & Sword titles please contact

PEN & SWORD BOOKS LIMITED
47 Church Street, Barnsley, South Yorkshire, S70 2AS, England
E-mail: enquiries@pen-and-sword.co.uk
Website: www.pen-and-sword.co.uk

Or

PEN AND SWORD BOOKS
1950 Lawrence Rd, Havertown, PA 19083, USA
E-mail: Uspen-and-sword@casematepublishers.com
Website: www.penandswordbooks.com

Contents

Acknowledgements

Once again, thank you Anne Coulson for checking my manuscript and to the staff at Reading Central Library for providing me original newspapers to work from.

Preface

This book is about Reading, regarded at the outbreak of the war as 'sufficiently far from London to be designated a "safe town" in the event of aerial bombing' – a view not necessarily shared by its inhabitants, as the town was an important rail junction. In common with many other towns in the south of England, the residents expected their homes 'to be razed to the ground by German bombers.'

It was the seat of a borough council, comprising Caversham, Coley, and parts of old Earley, Southcote, Tilehurst and Whitley, and was the county town of Berkshire. I have therefore occasionally included outlying towns and villages to provide a flavour of life in both rural and urban Berkshire during the war.

The narrative looks at local life from the immediate weeks before the war to the end of 1945 based on local history books and the weekly newspaper *The Standard*. This was the bestselling local paper and probably reflects best what was experienced in Reading. I have used mainly illustrations from the paper, although their reproduction was often very poor, as they do show what the reader saw and could gain from them.

Those who have read about Reading in the Great War will observe a considerable number of parallels. Indeed, in many cases only the names and dates are different. Similarly, there is a considerable overlap over the events of each year of the war.

Introduction

The Reverend Gibbs Payne Crawfurd, vicar of Sonning Church, wrote in the September 1914 Parish magazine that 'one thought dominates our minds. It is hard to think of anything else other than the war... any forecast maybe disillusioned by actual happenings. What must remain the same is the need for every man, woman and child among us at home to put their trust in God and go forward to meet the storm bravely and patiently, backing up the courage of our men on sea and land with their own grim determination to do and bear our part in the country's cause.'

In the October 1939 edition of the Sonning Church magazine, again the first after the declaration of war, The Venerable Richard Wickham-Legg, clearly feeling the same as his predecessor and having gone through it all before, expressed it more tersely: 'So the great tragedy has come upon us, and we are at War. A list of those serving in His Majesty's Forces will be found in another page. Let us remember them in our prayers, it is just the support they deeply value and appreciate.'

Woodley aerodrome before the war was part of RAF Training Command and on 3 September 1939 became No 8 Elementary Flying Training School, replaced in 1942 by No 10 Flying Instructors School. On the same airfield was the Miles aircraft company which produced aircraft throughout the war. In 1939 it numbered just over 1,000 employees but with the impetus of existing contracts and new work, numbers grew. Typical of the speed at which the company grew was the story of Jack Eyres of Henley, a skilled carpenter and joiner. The day after he was interviewed he was working full-time for the company. Skilled engineers and machinists were recruited from further afield,

Just days before the war began the local territorial battalion arrived back from their annual summer camp near Chichester.

including from other important industries like the railways. The need was continuous.

As the airfield was likely to be attacked, it was decided to move much of the work off-site. In late 1940 work was dispersed to premises around Reading; at its peak twenty-six other factories were involved in production. Other companies involved included Lewis' Yard in Vastern Road, Abbey Motors in King's Road, the Methodist Chapel in Castle Street, Serpell's in Liverpool Road (the most important satellite factory), Black's Stables in Earley, and factories in Henley, Princes Risborough, Willesden and High Wycombe. Later in the war, the company began manufacturing in Northern Ireland. By the end of the war it was employing several thousand workers, had repaired 3,000 planes and built over 5,000 in the main factory and two satellite plants in Marston and Doncaster.

During the Great War, the air raids on London had resulted in a mass exodus of Londoners to the safer area of the Home Counties. Reading had been one of those destinations, resulting in the town struggling to house the temporary residents, so many that police cells had to be used for overnight accommodation. It was the same in the second war.

The Reading National Service Committee warned the town's citizens in April 1939 that 'many thousands of people, particularly children', would flood the town if war broke out. Appealing to patriotism, they asked women to volunteer to look after unaccompanied child evacuees. Those who did not 'would be obliged to receive other billetees'.

Quickly the town became full and, in 1941, was closed: the first place to be officially classed as a 'Closed Town'. To control the influx, a Billeting Officer was appointed who gave permission for an outsider to take residence in the town and who had to be informed if someone left.

The number of inhabitants was increased not just by government evacuees; there were also a large number, estimated to be nearly as many as the official evacuees, who privately evacuated to Reading. Some also came to the town at the weekend for a rest. Many were transferred to the town from other parts of the country as war-workers, often with their families. A number of London firms moved their staff to Reading as did many government departments. The town was also the billet for a large number of troops and the normal camp-followers of any large body of men.

Basically there was a lack of accommodation; although there had been a number of new houses built before the war, any new building work was quickly curtailed due to shortages of labour and materials. One member of the council 'referred to the shortage as being colossal' and the council had tried to convince the government on 4 September to allow them to build 203 more council houses in Whitley. The proposal was rejected and following a further attempt in 1942 was rejected again.

Only a handful voluntarily evacuated themselves from the town: 'Several children and young persons of school age were sent to America by their parents.' Similarly, some families relocated to the West Country but returned when it became apparent that Reading was unlikely to be bombed.

Reading had been told to expect up to 25,000 evacuees from London: schoolchildren, mothers with children under school age, expectant mothers and the blind and crippled. This was 'too many' according to the Education Committee. 'Londoners had been settling in Reading since the Great War, and Reading itself was partly a "dormitory town" for London, because many white-collar workers commuted there for employment.' So it was felt that there would be a natural understanding between the residents and the wartime incomers. 'That understanding would be strained.' Mrs Marsh in London Road was one householder who certainly had this experience. She remembered that looking after four evacuee boys was 'very hard work, made harder by the frequent visits of their mother'.

The *Reading Citizen* offered the newcomers a warm welcome but added, 'It may seem Irish, but we hope their stay will be a short one.' It was not always a short stay. Tilehurst took its share of evacuees and some stayed after the war, married and settled there. Probably the strangest evacuee billet in Reading was in Tilehurst: three children and their mother were housed in a hay loft in the only house at the top of Cockney Green.

The peaceful village of Sonning was an obvious destination for evacuees. In October 1939 the vicar wrote that 'it was a great pleasure...to welcome the London children and their mothers and teachers' to the village where their presence brought joy.

In the three months before the war, 12,000 people moved into the town. By 1942 the town had grown by 40,000, the increase roughly split between official and private relocations. 'Nearly nine thousand households were served with billeting notices, requiring them to house incomers.' To provide extra accommodation, the newly constructed National Camps Corporation buildings at Kennylands, Kidmore End and Bishopswood Farm in Sonning Common were used. Reading's

The scale of the number of evacuees exceeded that expected but homes were found for them all. Here a group are leaving the station: each is carrying their gas mask in a small cardboard box.

'council estates were acutely affected', with the flood of immigrants being compared to pouring a quart into a pint pot. Somehow they were all found homes.

Among the new arrivals were 'enemy aliens', of which the town already had a number as permanent residents. They, like the new residents, many of whom were refugees from Nazi oppression, had to register with the authorities; their freedom of movement was curtailed and some were interned for the duration. As in 1914 there were issues with aliens, but in neither war were they a threat in Reading, more a problem to be contained. A number lived in the area, subject to the Aliens Order of 1939. They quickly disappeared but before that were an irritation, wasting police and court time. A typical example was Susanne Glatz, a middle-aged German cook, who moved from one registration district to another without informing the authorities.

With the increased population came a higher crime rate; the opposite of the Great War, when crime in general had gone down. There was not so much incentive for a black market in 1914-18 because few goods were rationed, but in the second it thrived.

The influx also put pressure on already nearly full local schools that with a rising birth rate would be become even fuller. With increased demand and a shortage of accommodation, a double-shift system of part-time education was operated by schools until early 1940 when full-time education resumed. Earley St. Peter's was a typical school affected by the influx. To deal with the overflow of pupils, the old church hall and the Porter Institute had to be used to provide accommodation. Even then, a shift system had to be operated with locals in the morning and evacuees from Battersea in the afternoon. The school itself was initially taken over by the local Air Raid Precautions Unit but, apart from one room of ARP material left behind, they moved out during 1940.

Unlike the last war, when the closest Reading came to an air raid was the glare of a burning Zeppelin over north London, Reading was a potential target. It was an important rail centre; in the town were a number of engineering works, all of which produced materials for the war effort; on the outskirts was an aircraft factory and airfield. It was also easily visible from the sky; planes simply followed the Thames or the rail lines from Paddington or Waterloo, all of which glittered in the moonlight.

Large organisations had their own fire guards and fire fighters. This is the lapel badge worn by ARP members at Simmonds Brewery.

Forward planning meant Reading was quite well prepared to cope with such an eventuality. Many houses had air raid shelters and there were communal shelters and aid posts across the borough. One public air raid shelter was constructed on the Royal Berks forecourt to hold 200 people. In the town centre shop basements had been converted to shelters and, in more open areas like Palmer Park and at Coley, deep trenches had been dug.

The directors of Sutton's Seeds had realised that war was a distinct possibility in May 1938 and began fire drills. Looking into air raid precautions for the company they took out insurance for £50 a year covering Sutton's for £100,000. They also granted special leave of absence to employees in the Territorial Forces to attend special courses as long as they could be spared from their work. Huntley & Palmers were also proactive and 'submitted to the Board of Trade a schedule of cakes and biscuits to be manufactured in wartime'. They also prepared for air raids by 'building…shelters and fitting dimmed lights in case of a black-out'. Repeating the benevolence shown their workers in the Great War, they 'reintroduced the principle of supplementing employees' pay while they were on full-time military or other national service'.

Sutton's took air raid protection and the war seriously and took a number of steps to safeguard people and property. 'Certain locations were designated as shelters, and sand-bags were to be filled for protection of the windows' in certain areas: the potato basement, pea store basement, loading floor and the basement under the front office.

Many men and women had volunteered for ARP work before the war to act as wardens and observers; anyone over the age of 14 was invited to join. In November 1938 the Reading branch was the first to train women as ambulance drivers and by the outbreak of war 180 drivers had been trained. Trained at Battle Hospital, 130 members of the WVS became nurses for the duration and over 100 worked for the Hospital Supply Depots at St. Mary's Church House and at 16, Northcourt Avenue. Air raid casualties would need hospital care and both hospitals were part of the Emergency Medical Service (EMS) set up by the government to deal with military casualties, if needed, and the hypothesised enormous number of civilian casualties caused by bombing.

As part of the EMS, Reading 'was notified that in the event of war it would receive some 400 patients to be evacuated from London hospitals, besides 25,000 children and non-combatants. This was different to the Great War when Reading was a military hospital, with small temporary convalescent hospitals set up across the town running alongside the two main hospitals.

The Women's Institute was also prepared. Although in existence since 1915, it ran its first meeting in Earley in March 1938. 'Many of their earlier activities were directed towards the war effort. They were soon not only having Keep Fit classes but also First Aid and Gas classes…to assist the local authorities with their ARP work.' Meetings continued throughout the war with the talks often reflecting 'important issues of the day, like Home Nursing, The Home Front, Evacuees Problems, Wartime Economies, and Poultry keeping'. Some were purely practical: making gloves, slippers, cookery and dressmaking; others were for interest, like those on holidays or 'The Adventures of a Suffragette'; some were debates: 'should double summer time be continued after the war?'

As during the Great War, the local Voluntary Aid Detachments of the Red Cross provided service, and even before the war some had gone to their war stations. On 15 August 1939 a telegram had mobilised the sixty-nine mobile members who lived in Reading and Berkshire: fifty-five went to hospitals in Aldershot, five to the RAF hospital at Alton and nine to the cavalry hospital in Windsor. Soon after, the rest were called up for local service.

The jobs they performed were myriad. Apart from assisting in hospitals, they opened a home for evacuee children in Caversham called Brooklyn, assisted local families trace relatives, helped with sending PoW parcels and provided 500 evacuees with clothing, bedding and temporary accommodation. They 'fitted 5,000 Contex filters to gas masks, and showed parents how to fit the special respirator hoods for babies'. Others helped

Women quickly played a prominent part in the war with many joining the armed forces. This is a member of the Women's Auxiliary Air Force.

on the Casualty Evacuation trains taking patients to Scotland. While in Earley, they 'cleaned and prepared a house requisitioned by the War Office for an ATS hospital [and] several detachments visited and cared for sick ATS women in their billets'.

During war, the ARP, later Civil Defence, received warnings about the possibility of a raid using a colour code: yellow – confidential preliminary warning with no action needed; purple – warning to extinguish all lighting; red – action warning on which sirens were sounded; and white cancelled all previous warnings received. This allowed them to alert the population to take cover. Across the borough there were sixty-four Wardens Posts, each equipped with a blast-proof telephone. In case of a raid there were ambulance depots, auxiliary fire stations, and rescue and repair parties.

The Auxiliary Fire Service was a voluntary organisation, although firemen were paid during the war. Firefighting was undertaken by men, with women working in control rooms and driving appliances, although after 1942 women received basic firefighting training. Reading was divided into six areas: central – Old Fire Station in St. Mary's Butts; south (actually two areas) – Gowring's garage in London Road; eastern – Thames Valley Garage on London Road; Tilehurst – Prince of Wales Pub; Caversham – Caversham Court. Other part-time stations were added during the war. In 1941 all the fire brigades were merged to become part of the National Fire Service (NFS), with Reading becoming 'A Division' of 15 Fire Force. To be certain of sufficient water, large tanks were set up around the town and natural water sources identified.

Although Reading was spared a major raid, people knew first-hand about the horrors of war. Local firemen were no longer local, being called to fight fires caused by raids across the south, bringing back stories of the destruction of Birmingham, Bristol, Coventry and Southampton. Also, many residents travelled to London on a daily basis and saw the realities of the German bombing campaign.

Along with high explosives, it was expected that the Germans would drop poison gas, so everyone was issued with a respirator, even new-born infants. Respirators were the most common lost property on Reading trams. If gas had been used, the Civil Defence authorities had decontamination squads to deal with it.

Many thousands flocked to join the civil defence: age was not a barrier. Here an elderly women poses in full uniform. Her helmet indicates she worked at a local First Aid Post.

Even though it was unlikely that Reading would suffer a major attack, The Royal Berks took sensible precautions to protect its valuable assets. Medical books from the library were despatched to Bradfield College. Specimens from the Hunterian collection of the Royal College of Surgeons, sent to Reading for safekeeping, were given to members of the medical staff to take away and look after.

The council had the same idea but dealt with it differently – dustbins. All its precious documents, including ancient charters, were sealed in dustbins containing a chemical to absorb moisture and hidden in the Emmer Green chalk caves. They remained there until recovered, in perfect condition, in July 1945.

Some men had been called up before the war, and many more received their call-up papers when war was declared. What was the same as the Great War was that local men disappeared from the town being replaced by men from other areas. It was different at Huntley & Palmers where the workers were classified as being in a reserved occupation and were not conscripted. Nevertheless, by 1943 the company workforce had shrunk to just over a thousand.

As in the Great War, there were those who did not want to fight, and hearings were set up to identify conscientious objectors. Again, as in 1916-18, there was opposition from those who felt it was the duty of every male eligible to serve to do their duty in the armed forces.

On the other hand, many young boys were keen to fight or serve in some other way. The authorities were quick to make use of the enthusiasm of the young by opening a register at the Town Hall for Boy Scouts who wanted to render national service.

They were also quick to make use of the enthusiasm of men who could not join the forces for whatever reason. Across the town, sites that were seen as the enemy's main targets in an invasion were, from mid-1940, to be guarded by the LDV, later the Home Guard. Sentries were to be seen at 'the river bridges, the railway marshalling yards, Brock Barracks, the Town Hall, gas and electricity works, and large factories such as Sigmund Pulsometer Pumps and Huntley & Palmers. At the Town Hall, sandbags were piled up around the building and armed men stood outside with fixed bayonets.'

The enthusiasm shown is clearly demonstrated by the story of one local man. He had volunteered for the army in 1914, lost a leg at Loos in 1915, been invalided out in 1916 and then joined the RFC as a cook until the end of the war. After further surgery on his leg he was one of the earliest recruits for the LDV. He then volunteered again for the RAF as a cook.

The experiences of the Earley Home Guard, a platoon of the Sonning Company, were mirrored across the town. It was based at a garage at Shepherds House Hill (presently the BP petrol station) which closed because of the fuel shortage. They kept themselves busy on a nightly basis, patrolling 'the railway line and bridges, Sonning Lock and the Gas Works'. Every member completed two patrols a week. On Sunday, the platoon met at the garage and marched to Company HQ at Blue Coat School in Sonning Lane where they trained and paraded. 'Training was rigorous, the men were required to keep fit and regularly attended a camp at Warfield on Saturday night. The following morning they had to run a tough army assault course.' They practised firing their weapons at Bisley or on the Downs near Didcot and regularly undertook an efficiency course in full kit with their rifle, when they had to fire '15 rounds from 500 yards in three minutes then to run 100 yards, lie down and fire another 15 rounds, again within three minutes and so on.'

Life in the Home Guard was essentially one of waiting and boredom. However, the men manning the 'rocket battery on the southern outskirts of the town were in action several times'. This was 101 Berkshire Home Guard 'Z' Battery under the command of Major Vanderpump.

By 1942 membership was no longer optional for men aged 18 to 51 in areas where the Home Guard was under strength.

Food control had a higher priority than in 1914 with the introduction of rationing early in the war. The production of many goods was controlled, with the war effort having first call on resources. Rationing was strictly enforced but not all foodstuffs were controlled. Money could still buy a better diet but in general everyone had enough to eat and wear. Many people enjoyed better health because of the control of their diet and the resulting reduction in their weight.

Providing ration books to the thousands in the town was made easier by National Registration which had been introduced in the Great War to find out how many men were available to fight. In the second war it was used in the same way but made the introduction of rationing more straightforward.

Petrol rationing for civilians really only affected those well off enough to own a car, but it had a great impact on delivery vans, the general movement of materials and goods, and of course public transport. Reading's buses were reduced to half services; fortunately the trams were not affected. To compensate for the reduced number of buses running, a greater number of standing passengers were allowed; even so, at rush hours there

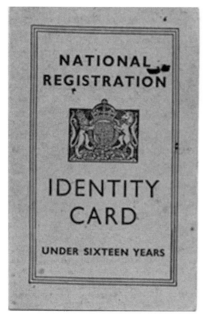

The National Registration card was introduced in September 1939 and had to be carried at all times by anyone aged 16 or over. Parents were responsible for their children's cards, even if they were not with their children.

was still insufficient space for all the passengers, many of whom had to walk considerable distances if their bus had already serviced too many stops. The effect of this reduction was felt most by the villages across Berkshire. Petrol rationing also put many commercial travellers out of work. For the well-off there was always the taxi, the price of which quickly rose from 8d to 1s a mile. For those whose work required them to drive it was possible to get extra coupons. On the positive side, a lack of petrol meant a reduction in traffic offences.

The situation for those used to a personal laundry service was explained in an advert from the West Reading Laundry in Wilton Road who still asked customers for their vans to call:

> *NOTICE Owing to the rationing of petrol and commandeering of transport it is only possible for our vans to make one call per week in Reading and District, when*

we propose to make a simultaneous collection and delivery.
We shall endeavour to give our many customers the best
possible service under present conditions.

Gowring's, that had already lost staff to the armed forces, told readers that although service had been curtailed they would continue to do their best, and that there were stocks of new vehicles available.

Vehicles were quick to convert to the use of kerosene but this was also in short supply. The use of coal gas created some strange and un-aerodynamic vehicles: the gas bag was fitted on top of the vehicle in a frame for protection. Converted vehicles had a very limited range and by 1942 had almost disappeared.

Money was key. People were asked not to waste it on frivolous purchases but to invest it in the war effort through bonds. As well as the national drives, on a local level War Savings groups were set up across the town, each with their own savings targets.

Naturally, established and new charities wanted their share. As in the Great War, flag days proliferated and there were regular special days/weeks when money was raised for a specific focus: Warship Week, Wings for Victory Week and Salute the Soldier Week. For the latter fundraiser, Earley St. Peter's school raised £615.

There were many smaller organisations that benefited from Reading's generosity. Throughout the war there were regular house to house collections for organisations like St Dunstan's for the Blind or the Aid to China Fund. Further money was raised by local whist drives, bring and buy stalls, and raffles.

Reading's hospitals relied on such collections. The Royal Berks had a Special Needs Committee that raised large sums through a regular Sunday Parade, flag days and other events. People were always asked to dig deep. As there was little to buy because of shortages, this was perhaps not such a sacrifice as it might have been.

Organisations like the Earley Women's Institute regularly contributed food and money to the hospital. A competition to grow the heaviest crop of potatoes from seed potatoes provided yearly resulted in the hospital receiving up to two sacks-full. 'Money from the egg collection and the annual New Year Party were also sent to them.' They also collected and sorted stamps for the hospital's appeal.

Not only money was needed. Churchill had said in May 1940 that he had nothing to 'offer but blood, toil, tears and sweat'. As the war progressed more and more people gave their blood to save the lives of others. Hundreds responded to simple appeals put out by churches and other organisations. 'Donors of blood are urgently needed for supplies to the troops at home and those abroad, for civilian hospitals and R.A.F. Stations.' Potential donors were informed that giving blood was quite painless. At the Royal Berks, the blood donors list increased to 180, and by the end of the year 1,576 people were on the emergency donors' register.

Hospitals also needed dressings. The League of Remembrance provided the Royal Berks with thousands in every year of the war.

It was a priority to prevent waste of resources. Reading people began to save everything that could be reused or recycled. Children took their part, collecting metal for smelting, paper for pulping, and glass bottles and jars for reuse. As in the Great War, to save paper, fewer, thinner, newspapers were printed.

Food waste was discouraged at every level. Recalling the Great War, in April 1940 groups across Reading learned of a government initiative to turn surplus fruit into jam, if there was enough sugar available; and there was the perennial question: was a marrow something that should be turned into jam?

That life did continue with a semblance of normality is shown by Harvest Festival and the continuation of church services throughout the war, albeit at different times because of blackout restrictions. From October onwards, the Evensong, just one of the services affected, was held in late afternoon. As in the Great War, churches across the town and county continued to hold an annual religious observance of the opening of hostilities.

Horticultural societies continued to hold their annual shows. These could be easily turned into fund-raising activities by a change of title, for example, the Victory Produce Show in aid of the Red Cross in August 1943.

As a practical way to help, people were encouraged to knit. 'A number of clothing articles have been knitted by parishioners,' wrote the vicar of Sonning, 'and have been gratefully acknowledged by the [Seaman's] Mission; 17 pairs socks, 2 pairs steering gloves, 2 pairs cuffs, 1 scarf, 1 pair sea boot stockings.' Knitting for those on active service continued throughout the war. The Earley WI, in response to a *Daily Sketch* appeal, sent twenty-one pairs of socks, two scarves, seven helmets, six pairs of mittens, two pairs of gloves and one pullover. And, when Europe was being liberated there was a need for clothing, so once again the ladies of the Earley WI busied themselves and produced 12 shawls, 24 coats, 24 pairs of knickers and 24 pilches (vests).

To assist service personnel, the town set up an Army Comforts Depot. By the end of hostilities it had supplied '1.25 million wartime comforts, ranging from mouth organs to helmet mufflers.'

Reading, like the rest of the country, began to black-out on 1 September, some time before there was any danger. And, as in the first war, Reading was not very good at it. There were hundreds of prosecutions for breaching blackout regulations in the first year alone; but the number decreased later in the war. The times of the blackout were given in the weekly papers so there were no excuses for not knowing.

The blackout made the sky darker, and the anti-aircraft fire over London could be clearly seen. 'Walking home from Marlborough House it was possible to watch the London searchlights and see the lights when the bombs dropped in London,' recalled Jean Gould. The blackout also saved the council money, £5,000 in just six months, allowing them to keep the rates at the same level in 1940. In the same edition of the *Daily Sketch* it was reported that, nationally, 1,200 people had been killed in road accidents in the previous month, many a result of the blackout.

Some changes were inconvenient or smacked of the government meddling in people's pleasures: early closing of shops made life difficult and the closure of the town's cinemas and its football club restricted people's leisure options. The ban on the cinema and football was temporary, and games were played, often to crowds of 20,000, throughout the war. There was no regular team because of conscription, but professional players stationed nearby played for Reading. Two notable players were Frank Swift, Manchester City and England goalie, and Matt Busby, future Manchester United manager.

Although hard, life was not without fun and laughter. Sue Hanscomb provides some typical examples of how Tilehurst enjoyed itself. 'Plays were performed at Westwood House and performed on the Rectory Lawn in the summer. Pantomimes were also performed,' even though it was summer. 'A tent was put up in the Rectory ground by the YMCA for the entertainment of troops from Ranikhet Camp.' Some 1,600 people in 1941 watched a concert at which the Royal Berkshire Regiment band played and the Irish tenor John McCormack sang, followed by community singing. It raised £129 for the Red Cross. This was a generous gesture by the regiment, given that it could have used the money to provide goods for its own PoWs.

Other simple pleasures included paying sixpence to dance to music on a wind-up gramophone or a trip to the cinema. As buses finished at 9 pm; this meant a walk home in the dark or leaving before the last show finished.

There are always casualties in a war but the papers did not carry such long lists of the fallen as they had between 1914 and 1919. With the commencement of hostilities, casualties appeared in the papers again.

That this was a different war is clearly shown by the Home Front propaganda; by 1944 the home front had become the Second Front. In the Great War there were no worries about Fifth Columnists and the threat of spies was well under control. In the second war, national security and the threat of idle chat became obsessions; 'Walls Have Ears' became a catchword. Gossip about war-related topics could, the posters suggested, lead to the death of loved ones.

Not everything changed during the war. Sutton's Seeds, a beneficent employer, kept jobs open while the men were away. On their return they quickly slid back into their positions, often with no change, as former office boy John Cox recalled. Having left the firm in 1939 a single man, when called up in the Territorials he had not returned for six years. When released from the army in May 1946, he was married, had no home, no money and his wife was expecting their first child. On his return to Sutton's, he found his old 'desk had remained untouched; even the pens were in the pen tray!'

The End of Peace in Reading

After the Munich Crisis of September 1938, Reading had slowly geared up for the war that many felt was unavoidable. Many had joined the ARP – Air Raid Precautions; work had begun on building air raid shelters and, in the weeks preceding the war, reservists had been called up, and men for National Service. Much of the news in the local papers was little different from that of 1914.

In the days just before the war, confusion about blackout arrangements between the RAF and the ARP resulted in the postponement of the Reading ARP 'war-time' exercise. It was held the next night, providing realistic search and rescue scenarios. 'Although no sirens were sounded, realism was imparted to the exercise by collapsing the interior of a house in Diver Street, one of a number previously condemned in a clearance area, and the rescue and clearance squads worked amid the fallen brickwork of the wrecked rooms, rescuing dummy "casualties". Detonators had been exploded to give the effects of bombs dropping.' Reading was prepared for the worst. In the reinforced basement of the Town Hall was a report centre; in Silver Street was a first-aid post with two ambulances and in the old Corn Exchange there were 'thousands of pounds of materials, including 600,000 sandbags'.

A week later the public were asked to pay attention to the four public information leaflets delivered to every house in the town, especially pamphlet number 2 which dealt with the masking of lights in the home. Air raid sirens were manned day and night, but wardens were not yet on standby. In case the situation escalated, there was a call for more volunteers to join the ARP.

Reading was classed as a safe town and no teachers were recalled from their summer holiday, but in London and other major cities they were told to report to work the next day, a Saturday morning, in view of the situation abroad. It was not an evacuation, just a readiness precaution in case war broke out.

The 4th Battalion (Territorials) Royal Berkshire Regiment had recently returned from its annual camp, as had the Berkshire Yeomanry; it was no longer a mounted unit but a Royal Artillery Battery. Unfortunately, at around 600 in strength, the 4th needed to recruit. Much of the time at camp had been spent in rain, but fortunately when the East Ward of the Reading Conservative and Unionist Association went for a day-trip to the coast, the sun shone.

In the days before the war, Reading hosted members of the International Friendship League. Five countries were represented but there was no one from Germany.

The Land Army was re-formed in June 1939 and volunteers were under training at the start of the war. The Faculty of Agriculture and Horticulture was one of the twenty centres where they were receiving instruction.

The papers contained the usual stories of crime and death. Walter Annetts of Bryanstone Square pleaded guilty at Reading Borough Police Court to 'being drunk while having the charge of two children apparently under the age of seven years'. Reading County Magistrates were dealing with the rights of mushroom pickers on private land who were causing problems in Swallowfield and damage to a noticeboard in the field. More seriously, the Reading coroner concluded that the baby wrapped in paper and dumped in a ditch had been murdered, and in Newbury the coroner was inquiring into the accident at the Kintbury railway crossing in June when Mr and Mrs Jennings of 174 King's Road lost their lives and their daughter and her uncle were seriously injured. The crossing at Kintbury still claims lives today.

There was a story of heroism. 'Olive Marks, a pretty fair-haired, blue-eyed little girl' who went to Newtown School was lucky to be alive to experience the war. Unable to swim, she had fallen into the River Kennet, but Greta Bakkers, a 14-year-old schoolgirl who was with her, jumped in and rescued her.

And there was a complaint. Men called up for the militia were not allowed to have their army pay made up to their civilian level by the council they worked for, but those serving in the Territorials, reserves and auxiliary forces, could. They were rebelling against government restrictions on top-up pay. There was call for equality of treatment, even though it would cost councils more to implement.

Papers made much of their money from adverts. What adverts was Reading looking at? For the well-off there was the possibility of a new car as the 1940 models were now arriving in the showrooms. A new Rover would cost between £275 and £360 at T. Baker in Friar Street. Or perhaps they might want to invest in property: the Aldermaston Court estate of 2,509 acres was to be auctioned in 394 lots. As well as the mansion, the vicarage, school and inns were also available.

For those on more limited budgets, Charles Nunn, pawnbroker at 79 King's Road, was hoping to sell unredeemed pledges. He was offering suits, jackets, waistcoats, trousers, boots, shoes, quilts, table covers plus wedding rings, dress rings and new and second-hand clocks, vases and tea sets. And for those with time on their hands, Watts & Co of Friar Street had a great variety of good and cheap fishing tackle; they could also provide guns and cartridges. Cashing in on people's worries about the possibility of war, Huntley & Palmers extolled their Krispbread, at 2 shillings a soldered tin, as the ideal Emergency Bread.

As in August 1914, the local travel companies were offering trips by coach to the coast and more local destinations ranging from exotic Bognor Regis to the 2 shilling Mystery Tour. On 3 September, for those prepared to rise early, there was a combined coach and steamer excursion to Ramsgate for 16 shillings leaving at 7 am, or for those who did not want to rush, at just 2 shillings there was a ride out to Streatley Hill and Whitchurch leaving at 6.45 pm. The next day, presumably for those who did not work or were on holiday, there was the option of two day trips for just 2 shillings: St. Giles's Fair at Oxford or a day at Northolt Park races.

Reading had a number of cinemas. The Granby billed itself as the town's luxury picture house and in the run-up to the war was showing two record-breaking films in one programme: *Convict 99* starring Will Hay, and a Hitchcock film, *The Thirty-Nine Steps* with Robert Donat and Madeleine Carroll. They boasted a lounge café, free cloakrooms and free deaf aid sets.

While people were free to go on trips and enjoy the cinema, the government issued advice regarding vehicle lights. The requirements were complicated, were often to prove dangerous, and sometimes lethal. With some light removed and the remainder fully masked to produce only a small amount of light, driving in the dark was going to be difficult.

Fortunately the war started the day after the South Reading Carnival. A day earlier and it could have ruined a lot of hard work by Gwyn Roberts of Linden Road. By selling more tickets for the carnival than anyone else, a whole £1 more than her closest rival, she was to be crowned Queen of the Carnival. There was also time to hold the Wargrave and Shiplake regatta, noted by *The Standard* as one of the most popular social events of the summer.

The last issue before the war, 1 September, contained a story of terrorist activity. Inspector Barker of the British Police Force in Palestine was killed on 26 August when a time-bomb exploded at his home in the centre of Jerusalem. It also carried notice of the government's intended evacuation arrangements on the day they had already commenced. Of the half-million Londoners expected to leave after 1 September, Reading Council was told to prepare for 25,000 evacuees, 'of whom 12,000 were to be children under five, with their parents, and 12,000 school children with teachers' most from elementary schools. However, in the same article readers were told to expect 43,000 people, of whom 12,000 were children. Importantly for many residents, it meant going to work earlier, as after 9.30 am most of the Corporation's buses were needed for the evacuees. In reality there was no problem with the arrangements and people got to work on time. Just after 10 am the first evacuees arrived.

The Mayor understood that this arrival would not be easy and made a statement about the evacuees. 'I feel that this billeting is an essential part of the national effort, and no matter how trying we may think it to have our homes invaded, we are as individuals playing our part. There is no need to stress the humanitarian side of it. If we are to be a united nation we must be united in everything.'

Gearing up for a war, two new territorial units were to be raised in Berkshire, an anti-aircraft battery and a medical unit. They were hoping that older men, normally excluded by age, would volunteer. If not in a reserved occupation, men aged between 21 and 38 could enlist at St. Giles's School for the newly formed Labour Companies of the Royal Engineers. Women aged between 18 and 43, up to 50 with previous service, were wanted for the Women's Auxiliary Air Force.

Reading's anti-aircraft defences were part of the Basingstoke Gun Defended Area. The guns were manned by Territorials and were part of the 5th Anti-aircraft Division controlled by the army with headquarters in Reading. Control of the guns passed to the Home Guard and women of the Auxiliary Territorial Service (ATS) operated rangefinders and searchlights. As the town was not considered to be a priority target, it was not until 1942 that Reading was defended by two half-batteries of four 3.7 inch guns. In 1941 decoy sites were set up around the town 'to create the impression of a target under attack'. Whether they were ever used is unclear. There was also an army camp on the site of the South Reading leisure centre which was later used to house PoWs.

The Red Cross was also appealing for more volunteers and the Mayor sanctioned the setting up of Citizens' Advice Bureaux which would need manning by skilled and experienced volunteers. A list of the Head Wardens in the town, along with their addresses, was also published. And, as was usual every week, there was a list of the dogs found by the police that were waiting collection, homing or euthanasia.

The next issues of the papers were five days after the declaration of war and by then it was old news so it did not appear until well into the paper. In *The Standard* it read in large bold letters: War declared against Germany. 'The declaration of war was heard by the people of Reading calmly and for the most part in their own homes. It came to them over the air and occasioned no surprise after the announcement at 10 am'. Those gathered in the town centre expressed a feeling of relief at the removal of uncertainty. In the evening, the King asked everyone 'to stand calm, firm and united in this time of trial'. Some people described this new war 'as the second edition of the first Great War to end war'.

The vicar of St. Peter's announced the news at the start of his service as did the Reverend Babb at Queen's Road Wesley Church. At St. Giles, the Reverend Bonsey emphasised the importance of carrying a gas mask and urged the congregation to help make the evacuees as happy as possible, while at the Wycliffe Baptist Church the Reverend Willis offered prayers of a character suitable to the circumstances. He curtailed the evening service to allow people to get home early.

The reception of the news was in contrast to the same news twenty-five years earlier. Then there had been clamouring for newspapers and large crowds gathered in the town. There was an air of excitement and an expectation of a quick victory. The second time there were just small crowds and the special editions of the papers were 'received without demonstration'.

By November the town's requirements for 4,000 babies' gas helmets and 3,000 children's respirators had not been met. Although they were supposed to have been issued to all, T.S. Hawkins was complaining that they were not available in Woodley because they had run out.

Police informed householders to make sure they blacked out sufficiently well, because from now on they would be taking drastic action against those who did not comply.

CHAPTER ONE

1939

Even with the constant threat of air raid, life continued almost as normal. People went to work, gardened, went to church, walked the dog and the Women's Institute ran their monthly meetings. However, the war quickly insinuated its way into everyone's life, even backwaters, as evidenced by the Sonning Parochial Church Council report for 1939: 'The war, which has been forced upon us, has, of course, affected us as well as the rest of the nation.'

Perhaps the war was the reason the number of entries was half that of 1938 at the Coley Allotment Holders' annual show; but the quality 'was well up to the average'. The war was certainly responsible for the Wokingham Show being held in camera: 'in view of the National Emergency, everything that is possible should be done to encourage increased production.' 'In spite of Hitler' and the war, Reading Repertory Company decided to keep going throughout the war.

An early casualty of the war was mail. Owing to the numbers called to the colours it was 'necessary to reduce the number of deliveries in Reading to two a day, commencing at 7 am and 3 pm'. The Head Postmaster reported the postal, telegraph and telephone business very busy. Much of this increase was mail for troops at home and abroad. To help goods going abroad, the Post Office recommended strong double cardboard boxes, wooden boxes, or several folds of stout packing paper, and as extra protection an outer covering of linen, calico or canvas, securely sewn up.

As a public safety measure places where a large number of people congregated were closed. The ban was short-lived; this is the Granby which opened on a Saturday after being closed for a week. Cinema going was popular as can be seen by the length of the queue.

Some of those conscripted did not wish to go. On 3 September, reservist Stanley Armstrong had had enough and returned home to Ashburton Road. He did not deny being an absentee: 'Yes, I suppose I am...I am not eligible as a Reservist as I am in receipt of a disability pension. I made a false declaration on my application form.' He was retained in custody pending a decision.

Regardless of personal choice, the call-up continued in age groups. On 1 October the National Service (Armed Forces) Act was signed. 'All male British subjects within Great Britain who are not already registered under the Military Training Act and who, on 1 October had not attained the age of 22, with certain exceptions,' were required to register on 21 October.

Some Christians were having problems about being involved in the war. The correspondent 'Interested' wondered whether the British belief in the righteousness of their cause was hypocritical and how they could pray to God to help them exterminate their brothers regardless of race. Was modern war a force for good?

In November *The Standard* carried brief stories about some local conscientious objectors. As in the Great War, they went before a tribunal that heard the evidence and then passed a judgement. John Caffyn told the panel that war was mass murder and the fact the Great War had not stopped further wars proved the bankruptcy of the war method. He was exempted from military service and told to take up agricultural work. R. Kyme, a telephone engineer, stated that in the light of Christian teaching it was impossible for him to take part in war. As his work for the GPO helped the military, he was told to join the RAMC as a non-combatant. No judgement was given for C. Hammond, but Mr Harbord, who appealed on the same Christian pacifist grounds, was exempted provided he continued his active social service for his fellow men. Unfortunately for them it was only a test tribunal.

A real appeal featured in the same edition. George Andrews from Wokingham, a 21-year-old laundry worker, applied for complete exemption as it was God's role to control life and that no war had led to a lasting peace. He offered to work in agriculture or with the Friends' Ambulance Unit but preferred to stay at the laundry. He was given three months to find a replacement and to be either employed on the land or with an ambulance unit. Later in the month a meeting of Reading and District Pacifists argued that non-cooperation and agitation against the war could stop it.

Harry Spenceley of Lennox Road appealed and was given leave to work in forestry if a position could be found. Charles Hammond, a university student, was registered unconditionally as a conscientious objector because of his strict pacifist views.

However, a fellow student with pacifist views was registered as a conscientious objector only while he remained a student. Gordon Wilson from Tilehurst was registered unconditionally as a conscientious objector, as was Maurice Tweedie of Conisboro Avenue, but only while he continued his work of national importance – the treating of cancer by radiological means. Agricultural student Douglas Snow was placed on the conscientious objectors list, but only while he was a student and so long as he went into agriculture after completing his studies.

How important tobacco was to the troops is clearly shown by a piece in December. 'Marked "Urgent," a folded pencil note was picked up off the platform at Reading G.W.R. station… "To Stationmaster Fenner," it read, "Reading Standard – Any cigarettes, etc., very gratefully accepted and acknowledged by 111077 Lce.-Corpl Appleby, R.A.S.C., No. 1 Petrol Base Coy., Army Post Office, B.E.F."'

The Women's League of Unity took out an advert telling everyone that the war had been forced upon the world by men. They wanted women across the world to unite to bring about the end of the war by winning it, and for it to never happen again.

The Co-operative Wholesale Society belatedly offered married men who worked for them 'the difference between the amount of their normal weekly wages and the amount of their service pay plus dependants' allowances, plus 15s (representing the estimated value of food, clothing, etc. supplied by the Government)'. A minimum allowance of 10s per week was to be paid and for single men a 5s payment was to be given if there were dependants. Many firms had done something similar before the war started.

Churches collected the names of locals on war service to include in their prayers. Harvest festivals went ahead: 'War, or no war, we are duty bound to thank God for the gifts of the Harvest,' wrote the vicar of Sonning. War intercession days were held in churches across the town, and of course the religious holiday of Christmas was kept.

Schools were affected. Taking Shinfield Road Council School as typical, it opened on 28 August to find that many children were away on holiday. After just a week, it closed for a fortnight on the declaration of war to work out how Reading was to cope with the expected influx of refugees.

Christ Church School had a similar experience. It closed on 1 September, but for a different reason: it was earmarked to be a Distribution Centre in the Reading Evacuation Scheme. It reopened on 18 September on half timetable; but unlike many other schools it was back to normal just a week later. The Junior Mixed and Infants' Department closed until 18 September to act as a reception centre for evacuees. When it opened again as a school, local children attended for the morning and in the afternoon it became Eltringham Street School for Infants from London, a situation that lasted until April 1940 when the Londoners moved to St. Luke's Sunday School buildings. In total, children from thirty-nine south London schools were evacuated to Reading, and some from Surrey.

Wilson School, a military hospital in the first war, was to become one again in the second, because it was close to Brock Barracks. 'The South and West Blocks were to be requisitioned while the North Block would remain in use for normal school purposes. A suitable barrier was erected to divide the site.' The pupils were taught in buildings close to the school. Like other schools they also had to cater for evacuated children.

On 31 August, the Junior, Central and Senior departments of Wilson School were requisitioned by the army and the children were given the school's equipment to take home. The junior school staff then transferred to Battle to assist with the billeting of women and children from London. The Infants School continued to run as normal until evacuee children reduced their attendance to a half day, but the Central and Senior went onto half timetables straight away. Accommodation for the juniors was found at Grovelands Baptist Church Sunday School Hall.

The evacuees were indeed a problem. 'In the first two weeks of September, Reading received approximately 13,000 "evacuated persons" about 9,500 of them children. All were to be allocated lodgings and the children were to be allocated to schools.' While Reading received all its allocation, Wokingham received just over half its allocation. Over 1,000 arrived in Bracknell and were given accommodation in the town, Chavey Down, Warfield and Winkfield.

But the Board of Education had planned well for the number arriving and all went smoothly. On arrival 'the evacuees were entertained in parks and swimming baths until the allocation job was complete.' Marjorie Culham of Earley remembered the new arrivals. 'I took my car to St Peter's Hall to help with the evacuation, and could have wept to see small primary children arriving clutching their luggage and iron rations – a tin of corned beef and a bar of chocolate and sundry other groceries. We took the children to various billets round the village.' The next day mothers with under-fives arrived. 'Billeting these was far more difficult.' The local WI had formed a Red Cross detachment and members assisted with canteens and sewing parties for evacuees and their parents.

The plan had not foreseen contagious diseases like impetigo which had to be isolated. The solution was to use Whitley Special School but this meant the 150 pupils had no school to attend; they had had no formal education since July. At the end of November the council were trying to find a house for the worst cases.

Driving a car at night continued to be problematic. The government came up with a compulsory kit and driving without the correct lights could incur a fine and cause death. Leslie Morgan of Oxford Road was knocked down and killed walking on Twyford bypass at night. He had been involved in an accident and had no lights so had left his car to find a phone box to seek help. A few weeks later, again at night, on the same road, Able Seaman Hasker of Blandford Road was killed on his motorcycle when he collided with a stationary lorry.

How genuine this 13-year-old evacuee's comments were and how locals took them is unknown: 'After spending two weeks as an evacuee in Reading I can only say that we are having a far better time than I expected. My host and hostess and all the people I have met have been so kind and helpful that I have had no time to get home-sick…evacuation is more like a holiday…

of course, Reading is quieter after London but I like the country atmosphere.'

War seems to bring out a need in some people to write poetry. The relationship between many of the evacuees and their new parents is perhaps typically described by an anonymous poem in *The Standard*:

Earley was in days of old a peaceful Berkshire Village,
But now they've sent from London Town a taste of dirt and pillage.
We must be just, and so we say that of the children sent
The great majority aren't bad, although our days are spent
In washing, mending, making clothes, for toddlers and others
Who have come down with scarce a rag, to live with Foster Mothers.

Evacuation days are done – at least we hope so truly –
But still we're hearing of the few who are somewhat unruly.
Unruly children can be trained, although the task is hard –
Some are not even house-trained and would foul and spoil a yard.
But still we all must do our share, and when they leave the house
We clear up after them and smile, and quite forget to grouse,

For some of them are lovely kids, and joy it is to hear
A Foster-Mother who can say "My new son is a dear!
Of course, he makes a lot of work, but I love him more each day
And shall really be quite sorry when he has to go away!"
If only we can do our bit, and grin – when all is told
Then Earley will be peaceful, as it was in days of old!

The sudden influx swamped schools; staff had to work shifts to accommodate the extra children. Fortunately their teachers also came, so teaching was shared. Shifts created 'off' which concerned many adults. 'The Head Teachers in the Borough wrote jointly to the Education committee expressing their concern about the 'off' sessions.' Their concerns were serious: 'Unless measures are taken to instruct and occupy pupils during their 'off' sessions, the effect on them will be deplorable, both emotionally and morally.' This issue was again raised later in the war.

Phoebe Cusden, a labour councillor, recorded her concerns in 'Juvenile Delinquency'. She emphasised the 'absence of fathers; mothers working; loosening controls'; loosening at home and at school caused by short time, the shortage of staff and even larger than usual class sizes. Cusden noted other factors that affected the young: 'mental deficiency, mental dullness, lack of opportunities for leisure, the growth of petty theft and violence among children'. She was also concerned about them playing football in the streets.

A solution was found. Reading's churches offered their buildings for free, as long as the Education Committee paid for heating, lighting and caretaking. This not only kept children busy, but also kept the locals away from the evacuees. In good weather, schools with a green space close by chose to use 'off' periods for walks and games for the children.

A further problem emerged. 'Children, many of whose fathers had been called up into the armed forces, found their insecurity increased by the loss of teachers for the same reason. The combined effects of the war on education in Reading..., were undoubtedly to lower the standard of work achieved... during the war.'

The new residents increased demand for goods, especially food, causing local shortages. There were grumbles about the cost of goods; one disgruntled lady, signing herself as HOUSEWIFE, wondered what the real cost of goods was (this was in an age of retail price control on many articles) and how could she find out? Reading in the papers that Dutch eggs were 1s 9d a dozen, why were they 11d for six in her local shop, and why was sugar a ½d for 2lbs more than the price in the morning paper?

The need for rationing was obvious, but it was months away, and later in the year the papers would report that there was no food shortage in the town. It was a case of eating what you could get or afford. October was national Doughnut month; the food was widely promoted as a breakfast item and was regularly served in schools and hospitals.

There was a shortage of air raid shelters, even though Reading had been building them for some time. Within six weeks of the start of the war, Shinfield Council School had a shelter which could accommodate 100 children or 80 adults but there was no lighting. There were more than a hundred children at the school but no further building was started until January 1940. With the frequent alerts they were regularly in use. Again like St. Peter's School it was used by the ARP; during the night fire-fighters slept in the building.

The council had carefully costed the need for the further construction of shelters and trenches at public elementary schools. Fortunately it was less than estimated at £37,500, of which half would be paid by the Board of Education.

To alleviate the shortage of household shelters, Reading Museum helpfully had a small model of an air raid shelter that could be constructed in a garden. In the first week of the war they modified the model and provided leaflets on how to construct it for around £3. With a five foot depth, some areas

An interesting exercise in stamina. To ascertain how far and at what speed they could travel wearing respirators and steel helmets, the ARP messengers of D Group had a test run to The Warren from the town centre.

of the town would have been digging in the water table, but if constructed following the detailed plans it would afford the occupants 'protection from blast, incendiary bombs, shrapnel and gas' (if respirators were worn). However, it was not proof against a direct hit. Full-size versions could be seen in local parks. One reason for the shortage was a lack of steel.

The number of communal shelters was boosted by a surprise discovery. Underneath Holy Trinity Church, Oxford Road, and next door at Jarvis's garage, there were enormous vaults, the latter protected by three floors of Ferro-concrete. At twenty-six feet underground, they were certainly safe. They were believed to be the result of chalk mining.

Another surprise was found at 7, Castle Street. 'Two workmen engaged in erecting an air raid shelter at the rear of the building' found a number of human skulls and other human bones. Some of the bones had been sectioned surgically, suggesting the work of a surgeon.' It was believed they had been disposed of by two doctors who had used the premises sixty years previously. Mr Smallcombe, the museum curator, shrugged the matter off: 'Human relics are always difficult to dispose of, and I suppose whoever put them in the hole in the garden at Castle Street thought they would be hidden for good.'

Reinforcing the view of Reading's country atmosphere, and also showing how different London was, is shown by a special exhibition at the museum. The evacuees caused anxiety over their lack of knowledge about what could be poisonous in a hedgerow, so a case of specimens to show which could be eaten and which were dangerous was put on display.

Concerns about shelter shortages were highlighted on 6 September. At 7.32 am, the first air raid sirens were sounded. 'Members of the public who were in the streets on their way to work went to the nearest shelter. Civil Defence personnel and police were on duty in the streets and stopped all cars and other traffic.' Ninety minutes later the All Clear was heard and 'there was a rush to get to work. Reading Borough Police Station was inundated with telephone calls, numbering nearly 1,000 asking for information.'

There were insufficient shelters in the town centre for the number of people who might be there during a raid. This was addressed by the construction of eight shelters in the Broad Street area with an ultimate provision for 15,000 people. The location of the new shelters was kept secret until they were all complete. This was to stop a mass rush on one shelter.

Their completion was two months late and not without peril to pedestrians. It was not the practice then to fence off construction sites or excavations and accidents were more common; the blackout was an added danger as Grace Emms of Church Road, Tilehurst, found on 21 November while attempting to catch a bus. She was admitted to hospital with severe leg injuries following a fall in Broad Street. At around 6.10 pm, attempting to get on the bus, 'she walked between two danger flags into a pit being prepared as an A.R.P. shelter.' The pit was 15-18 feet deep.

Meanwhile, the old tram lines across the town had not been filled in and were causing accidents; they were a particular problem to cyclists.

In only the second week of the war, three people were killed by buses, two on Broad Street and one on Peppard Road. Days later, 71-year-old Harry Jones was killed by a car as he crossed the road.

It was decided to periodically test the sirens in the town. The first test took place on 3 December at 1 pm with the intention of repeating the test on the first Sunday of every month afterwards. The test was in three parts: a steady note for 30 seconds – raiders passed; 20 seconds of Action Warning signal (warbling); and a steady note for one minute.

The first test highlighted the problems which were clearly described in the papers soon after. Like the air raid warning at the start of the war, there had been confusion with different sounds at the same time from different sirens; so much so, that in a real raid it could lead to loss of life. However, the ARP was satisfied with the test.

Residents were advised to take whatever precautions were possible. The simplest were to put tape across windows to reduce

Throughout the war civil defence teams held regular exercises so that in the event of the real thing they would know what to do. This is an early trial run.

flying glass, and to put sandbags on shelters; businesses piled them in front of vulnerable points. Filling them required a lot of sand but this was not a problem: the owner of a sandpit in the Reading area offered it free to those who could collect it, on the proviso that it could not be resold.

While many men had arrived in Reading from other army units, needing temporary billets, the local Territorials were stationed elsewhere. To help them, the Army Comforts Office, at 12, St. Mary's Butts, asked for money to buy duty-free tobacco and cigarettes. They also wanted mittens, mufflers, socks, helmets and pullovers as long as they were made of khaki wool. Chocolate in slabs in packets, tins of sweets, playing cards, razor blades, soap and shaving soap were also welcome. In the period between November and Christmas the depot shipped fifteen tons of woollen clothing to the BEF.

Money was also needed for animal welfare; Wokingham ARP ran a first-aid centre for animals that helped raise their own funds – dogs with collection boxes walking the streets.

Rationing began in September with the government Fuel and Lighting Order. This meant that coal, gas and electricity would be rationed and anyone using more than two tons a year needed to register with a coal merchant.

While the evacuees were being settled, and Reading was adjusting to the war, there came some serious news. Although it was a disaster at sea, it touched many homes in the town. While the casualty lists would never be as long as in the Great War, they would hurt just as much. On 17 September, HMS *Courageous* was sunk by U29. On board were a number of men from Reading and district, some of whom died. *The Standard* carried photos and stories about the survivors; one was just 16 and had been on the ship for two months. Fred Ball of Great Knollys Street was lucky to survive. He was on the flight deck when the order was given to abandon ship. He was being pulled down by the ship when he suddenly found himself on the surface and was able to grab a piece of wood to stay afloat.

At the same time as the sinking of the *Courageous* there appeared the first requests for people to be careful what they said. A coincidence? A small advert stated: '*WALLS HAVE EARS. There is too much talking! Information which might be of great value to the enemy is being passed on every day in hotels, public houses and general meeting places. Sailors, soldiers and*

Leading Supply Artificer John Brown, of 92 Wokingham Road, survived the sinking of the aircraft carrier Courageous.

airmen are forbidden to talk shop – why should you? It is every citizen's duty to refrain from discussing with their friends such information as movement and numbers of troops and the names and nature of units and stations. The enemy has a spy system. Chance remarks are often dangerous. Failure to comply with this request may result in severe penalties.'

A month after the loss of *Courageous* came news of the loss of HMS *Royal Oak*; a severe blow to the navy's morale and a severe blow to the Reading families who received news of the death of their sons. *The Standard* carried some of their stories and photographs. One was due to retire from the navy at the end of the month; one family received a letter from their son telling them he was well the day after official notification of his death; two friends from Tilehurst died together, one just 16.

Stories about individual casualties were reported. Pilot Officer Gordon Salmon of Belle Avenue was missing following an aerial engagement but, as he is not listed by the Commonwealth War Graves Commission, he was probably captured or turned up later. Flight-Sergeant Letchford of East Street was killed in a flying accident.

Reading Prison had been empty and allowed to fall into disrepair. However, such a large building could not go unused during a war and plans were made to restore it for use. A working party from Feltham Borstal arrived to clean it up. It was expected that spies and fifth columnists would be incarcerated there, but the first inhabitants were prisoners from Wormwood Scrubs brought in to act as firewatchers.

Reading boasted two hospitals which became part of the government's Emergency Medical Service. Organised on a regional basis, the aim was to meet the demands from air raids, refugees and hospitals destroyed in air raids. The government reserved and paid for beds. 'Reading was regarded as a key area, already coping with refugees from London and expecting tens of thousands more fugitives and casualties from air raids on the capital.'

Over 150 beds were reserved at Battle Hospital and arrangements were made to turn corridors and rooms into wards. 'Steel sheeting was supplied for the operating theatre roof and the theatre was protected with a wall of sandbags, filled by volunteer labour. The basement of the Nurses' Home and other cellars were strengthened to serve as shelters. A First Aid Post was established in the Out-patients Department, members of staff were formed into a Fire Brigade.' The ambulance was old and worn out so a new one was purchased.

Battle First Aid Post was one of seven across the town; they were constantly staffed and were there to treat the 'walking wounded' and those affected by persistent poison gases. The others were at Caversham Parochial School, The Laurels in Tilehurst, Grovelands School, the ARP Centre, Silver Street, Whitley Clinic in Northumberland Avenue and Newtown Infants School. To aid their work they had 50 ambulances and 33 cars staffed by over 250 female drivers.

The hospital was soon under severe pressure from extra patients – evacuees, service personnel and war-workers – and the call-up of staff: doctors under 41 were liable for military service but the council did at times refuse to release key workers for the forces. There was also the issue of extra pay, initially to attract new staff; it soon became expected because of the extra work being done. Eventually, as in the Great War, employees received a war bonus. Unfortunately this did not reduce the high staff turnover and by December 1941 there were only two staff nurses. It took pay rises matching salaries in other hospitals to halt losses and recruit new staff.

The shortage of doctors was solved later in the war by relaxation of the regulations on the employment of aliens. Four were prominent: Dr Blitsztejn (Polish), Dr Hausmann and Dr Strykes from Austria and Dr Grieffenberg from Germany. Later in the war, some aliens were forbidden to work in hospitals like the Royal Berks where they might come into contact with service personnel.

The Royal Berks as part of the EMS was quickly involved in the war. 'By September 3rd, 1939 the hospital had received 166 of the 400 London patients evacuated to Reading and the town itself began to receive the thousands of evacuees it had been warned to expect.'

Like Battle it underwent physical changes. 'Strapping was put on windows; sandbags, later replaced by blast-proof wall, protected the front entrance and ground-floor windows; the word 'Berkshire' was obliterated from the front of the building so that no useful information could be gained by enemy agents.' There was even a suggestion that the roof be camouflaged.

Hospitals need good ventilation and strong light, the latter causing immediate conflict between patient needs and the law. Attaining and maintaining an efficient blackout was difficult but achievable. 'Some windows were painted over and others were covered with thick curtains. Lights were dimmed and covered with dark shades.'

Both Reading hospitals gave instructions to patients and staff on safety measures to be taken in the event of air raids. The glass ceiling of the operating theatre was protected. Patients had their gas masks with them but those unable to wear them or those recovering from an anaesthetic were transferred to one of two gas-proof rooms: Huntley and Palmer and Albert Wards. In case of a gas attack, there was a decontamination unit in the Royal Berks Hospital forecourt. Also in the forecourt was a trench which contained the hospital's supply of light bulbs and the inflammable material normally kept in the dispensary.

And, in case a bomb hit the radium supply, it was sent to Mount Vernon Hospital in Northwood.

Both hospitals had ARP posts with a staff member as chief warden. At the Royal Berks the head warden 'was in charge of sandbagging and also supervised the squads of porters and works staff who had been instructed in firefighting. Regular blackout patrols were organised and during air raid alerts fire-watching duties were carried out using the tonsil ward…as a watch post and later a spotter's tower, specially constructed on the roof of Nuffield Block.' Naturally the celebrations planned for October had to be cancelled.

Although the bigger of the two hospitals, the Royal Berks only 'agreed to make 100 beds available for military and air raid casualties. Of these, 80 were to be kept empty and ready for emergency use and the other 20 would be capable of being vacated at short notice.'

The scheme was lucrative for both hospitals; they were paid for their availability and paid again when their beds were used. The payment included the treatment of service and civilians, the police, auxiliary services and schoolchildren evacuated from London. It allowed payments to be made to honorary medical staff. After much thought it was 'decided that Benyon Ward would be kept available for air raid casualties and other beds in the old building would be used for E.M.S. cases in preference to the new Nuffield Block'. Even with the new block, and transfer of London patients to other areas, there was still a shortage of beds for locals; by the end of the year the waiting list was 500.

The hospital was under pressure from the start of the war: 'the surgical lists were growing rapidly and in September 1939 it was noted that one operating session in the general theatres started at 8.50 am and continued until 7.30 am the following morning.' And that was only the first month of the war. Fortunately or not for those children scheduled for tonsillectomy, the King Edward Ward was made available so the surgery could resume.

The call-up resulted in a shortage of staff. Within weeks of the war starting, the Royal Berks lost the senior surgeon and anaesthetist, an ambulance driver, three stokers and the window cleaner. 'A great shortage of domestic and laundry staff developed', but 'on the wards help was provided by auxiliary nurses and V.A.D.s from the Red Cross.'

Many companies planned for a long war. Sutton's had plans to possibly close the London office and shop, blackout all windows, start the day earlier to use less artificial light, use torches in case of power supply problems, and remove colour from the catalogue which would have vegetables at the front. Four months before the war they had held classes on the jobs of the air raid warden, gas and decontamination and first aid. The firm's fire brigade was increased to 24 personnel, and 16 air raid wardens, 8 decontamination officials and 16 first aiders had been appointed. Following the government's directive further air raid shelters were constructed during late August and early September.

Test evacuations showed that all employees could be in a shelter in just three and a half minutes. This was not as good as the CWS printing works in Elgar Road. In a surprise practice a few days before the war, all '600 workers were in their underground shelters and the fire fighters and other personnel were at their stations within two minutes and a quarter of the alarm being given.'

With the outbreak of war, Sutton's set aside a room for sleeping so that the fire pump could be manned continuously. A year later young men with good eyesight, aided by binoculars, were stationed on the roof to comply with the government's Fire Watchers' Order.

The voluntary evacuation of the affluent parts of London such as the West End and Jewish residential areas such as Golders Green and North Hampstead swelled the number of residents in towns close to the capital. Though well off, these families were not quick to spend money if they didn't have to. Mrs West of Earley looked after four young evacuee boys from a well-to-do London family. The government paid her for everything for the first ten weeks; after that the parents had to contribute. When the government subsidy ended, the family collected their children and took them back to London.

Throughout the war, the Reading ARP HQ, later Civil Defence, received warnings about the possibility of a raid using a colour coding: yellow – confidential preliminary warning with no action needed; purple – warning to extinguish all lighting; red – action warning on which sirens were sounded; white – cancelled all previous warnings received. Fortunately most of the warnings, although causing alarms to be sounded, were for planes heading further inland. The sound of their engines was very clear and kept people awake, even out in the suburbs. Margaret Fairburn remembered: 'we sometimes lay in our beds listening to flights of German bombers droning overhead to the Midlands and returning in the small hours having caused untold suffering.'

With shortages came exhortations to dig for victory and rear poultry; there were no restrictions on keeping chickens in the back garden as today. What the government wanted was for every family in Reading to cultivate 10-pole of ground which would keep a family of four in vegetables for the year and might 'produce 220 days' food in a mixed diet for an average man doing a day's physical work'.

Many wondered where the land would come from. The council said there was plenty of land and there were already over 4,000 allotments in the town. They changed this to 6,262 available, hoping that by Christmas 5,000 of them would be tended. Areas of grassland in the town needed to be dug up to provide new allotments. The labour for this was free – senior school boys.

As well as the land shortage, there was a further problem. "RUN, RABBIT, RUN!" was a headline in *The Standard.* As a result of the rabbit epidemic in Berkshire, it was suggested that 'hundreds, one may say thousands of acres' would bear no crops until the rabbits were eradicated.

A few weeks later it was reported that they were no longer a problem. One landowner said that until recently he had 400 on his land, now there were only 25. He explained this by the price of a rabbit. 'When they were worth four pence each no one bothered about them, but now, with the price at eighteen pence each, everyone wants them.'

Taking notice of lessons learned in the Great War, people were quick to 'Dig for Victory'. These are boys from Alfred Sutton turning spare ground into an allotment. The shop fronts are not recognisable today.

Rats are always a problem, but during the war the problem was more serious. To reduce the damage they caused to food supplies, the week beginning 6 November was Rat Week War. Care of animals by the RSPCA even extended to rats. They asked people to kill the rats humanely, not in the callous way most people destroyed vermin.

The advent of food rationing was one of the reasons to grow your own. Getting ration books for a range of foods ready for a town the size of Reading was no easy task. It took a full week, and extra clerical staff, to prepare 120,000 books. Knowing how many to prepare was made easier by the use of the forms completed on national registration day – 29 September.

To show equality with the people, the King and Queen requested they be issued with ration books. They also requested ration books for all the royal household officials and for each of the 200 servants.

Clothing was not rationed. McIlroy's department store suggested buying clothes as a tonic that would allow the buyer to face their problems with a lighter heart. What more sensible attire could a woman wear than an outfit that could be quickly slipped on should there be an air raid at night: slacks and a jumper, both with zips for ease of fastening.

Air raid blackout continued to be more than just a fashion problem. Late in the year, George Moppett, a 70-year-old stable hand, was killed when he was knocked down by a pedal cyclist. A few days later, the clergy of St. James Church, Abbey Ruins, were 'mourning the loss of a very faithful friend…one of Hitler's victims' – Bruce the presbytery dog was killed by a car during the blackout.

Accidents also happened in daylight, like the death of 69-year-old Mrs Miles of Western Avenue in Woodley. As she cycled onto Butts Hill Road from Old Mustard Lane she was hit by a car. Mrs Froude blamed the death of her 3-year-old, hit by a lorry at a pedestrian crossing, on the daughter she said was always 'so daring'. And a local known as Banana Jack was killed by a cyclist.

Nationally, in October, only three children had been killed on the road during the blackout compared to 421 adults. However, in daylight hours 64 children had been killed compared with 84 adults; 43 per cent of daylight fatalities involved children under 15. Some deaths even happened on the pavement.

Animals could be dangerous, as 11-year-old Roy Slade found out at Reading Cattle Market. Entering a pen, the animal turned on him; he was taken to the Royal Berks suffering from injuries to the back of his head and a thigh. The same day a farm worker was kicked on the head by a horse and admitted to hospital.

In an attempt to make the roads safer, a blackout speed limit of 20mph was proposed until it was pointed out that the police would be unable to enforce it because it was too dark. Working on the railways at night was dangerous: Francis Birkett was crushed to death by two trucks he was attempting to couple in the dark.

The liberal use of white paint was seen as a possible answer. In October the town was informed that the ARP had large quantities stored, but no mention was made of how it was to be used or who was to apply it.

Offences against blackout regulations occurred regularly and were reported alongside petty theft, drunkenness and army absconders. One ironical prosecution was that of Councillor Edminson; he was the chairman of the council's Air Raid Precautions Committee. No doubt he received considerable ribbing at committee meetings for some time after. Just three weeks into the war, there was a long list of summonses at the Reading Borough Police Court, all of which brought fines of 10s, all for permitting light to be displayed. Messrs Baynes were found guilty of showing light through a skylight, Eric Hookway of Kingsbridge Road alleged the light seen was from candles, and one plaintiff claimed he was sleepwalking. A record six people in one sitting were fined at the end of October. A few weeks later, eleven were fined in one sitting.

In their defence came a ratepayer's protest from James Berry of Earley. He stated the obvious that was ignored by the authorities: '90 per cent of householders had nothing with which to darken their houses when the order for complete darkness was given. Since that time materials have been difficult to procure, and what are now obtainable cost about three times their proper price.'

There was more to this moan than the cost of blackout curtaining. The writer also complained, as in *Dad's Army*, about wardens who were rude and tactless. They needed 'forcibly reminding that a "tin hat" does not necessarily constitute a "tin god".' It was also intimated that they were drawing more than their fair share of expenses, especially those who did not need the money. The use of men and women approaching 70 as ARPs was also questioned, as they would most likely be of little use if strenuous effort was needed.

Possibly the most extreme blackout precaution was in Tilehurst. A milkman bringing the milk was surprised to see that the empty bottle to collect was shrouded in black, carefully fastened with a safety pin. Staring in amazement, an old lady's voice called through the window: 'It's all right, you can remove the wrapping. I put it on so that the moon should not shine on the bottle and give the show away if the air raiders happened to come.'

The blackout was especially difficult for the deaf. In December, they began to wear a luminous badge with DEAF written on it. This was to stop ill-feeling if a collision occurred in the dark and no apology was forthcoming, as well as to help deaf people when an air raid warning was sounded.

Beer was a major issue in the Great War and one that was also raised in the second. It took Reading drinkers a month before they made a comment about it. The extra penny tax would not achieve its aim of raising money, they said, as many would not be able to afford the price rise. The Exchequer on the other hand estimated the tax would raise £93,500,000 extra a year or approximately £250,000 a day. 'Therefore when we drink our glass of beer, whether it be ale or stout, mild or bitter, we are not only doing good for ourselves but we are cheerfully assisting the National Exchequer,' beer drinkers were told. The price of a small Guinness was either 7d, 7½d or 8d; J. Gough of Caversham Road wondered what the correct price was.

Opening times were not long enough for some and there was often a temptation to close the doors and continue in private. If the alcohol was free it was legal otherwise the landlord could be fined. During the Great War the licensee of the Allied Arms had been fined for contravening the Defence of the Realm regulations; in November 1939 the new licensee was also in the papers. He had been selling alcohol after hours and been caught red-handed by the police. His punishment was a £5 fine.

Reading's hairdressers had a similar problem. They had signed a petition asking the Mayor 'to invoke the clause in the

Order of Council…whereby shops' could appeal to stay open until 7 pm instead of 6 pm, if it was in the interest of the public. As most people did not finish work until about 6 pm it would be difficult for them to have a haircut if the barber was closed. They thought they could lose thirty per cent of their trade and would have to let some staff go. They wanted 7 pm closing and 8 pm on late nights.

Maintaining the hunt was also an issue. It had slowly disappeared in the last war because of the shortage of dog food and because horses were needed at the front. A mechanised army did not need horses, but there was a meat shortage. A further problem was that many of those who ran the hunts were soldiers needed on military duties. They decided to hunt for just two days a week; naturally it was not for sport but the good of the countryside, to keep it open and maintain a small pack of hounds. However, they hunted three times in the first week of October.

In their defence, Master of the Foxhounds H. Wynmalen of Twyford calculated that hunting generated £15,000,000 a year and was comparable with many other industries. If that much money was spent on hunting, the League for Prohibition of Cruel Sports wondered, might it not be better spent on increased farming or any other useful industry. It was contrasted against true sports: does a footballer kick a live ball; do boxers select a child or animal as their opponent? One letter writer compared the treatment of humans in Germany to the treatment of animals by English sportsmen.

By the end of the year people had got used to the blackout. But in December alone, the blackout was held responsible for the deaths of 895 people nationally, from a total of 1,155 road fatalities; compared with the December 1938 total of 638.

In November, Reading reported its September blackout accident totals. The figures were naturally higher than the previous year (in brackets) with 112 accidents (85), four persons killed (1) and 53 injured (29). All the fatalities and twenty-three of the injuries took place during the blackout. The total for the quarter was worse though: 14 killed and 549 injured in road accidents, most in 30 mph areas – perhaps this indicated some improvement. Reading apparently also had fewer casualties than other comparable towns.

It took until February of the next year for the government to come up with an appropriate slogan. It must have taken a lot of thought to come up with – "Look out in the Black-out!" There

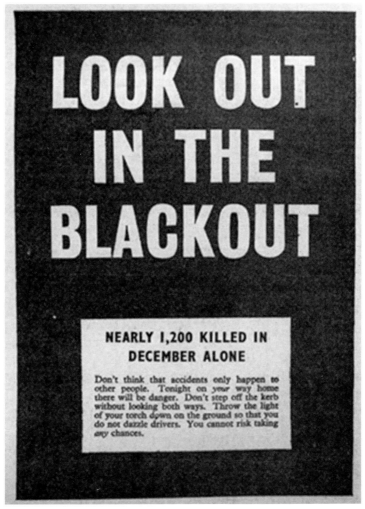

Across the country the blackout caused a range of problems. The most serious was the scale of road deaths. How serious it was is shown by the statistic in this government advert.

were evidently just four rules to ensure getting home safely in the black-out:

1. When you first come into the black-out, stand still for a minute to get your eyes used to the darkness.
2. Look *both* ways before stepping off the pavement. Make *sure* there is nothing coming.
3. Where there are traffic lights, always cross by them. It is worth going out of your way to do this.
4. Throw the light of your torch down on the ground.

At St. Laurence's Church on 29 October, 'for the first time in more than 800 years, no lights were to be seen twinkling through the stained glass windows.' It had covered all its windows to allow evening services to continue.

Crime continued: men assaulted their wives, people stole bicycles, drivers ran red lights and shopkeepers broke regulations by selling cigarettes out of hours. Harry Hudson of Armour Road was found guilty of assaulting his wife even though he claimed it was her fault and that she must have tripped over the dog and hit her face on the sink. After claiming his wife was vindictive and had been persecuting him for the previous six months, the chairman, Alderman Miss E.M. Sutton, told him that as he had been provoked he was to be fined only £5. Mrs Martha Larcombe from Burghfield admitted stealing a bike but was dismissed under the Probation of Offenders Act on payment of 15s costs. She had taken the bike because her husband was on short pay and she needed a job. Francis Dean of Caversham Road was fined £1 for selling cigarettes when his shop should have been closed for the sale of tobacco. A conman was in action in the Reading area pretending to collect money for the purchase of cigarettes for the troops abroad. Whether or not he was apprehended was not mentioned.

A 10 November headline read, 'Shoplifting must be stopped'. Over the weekend four cases of thefts from Reading stores had been heard at the police courts. The chairman of the Monday Bench indicated that 'there was a great deal of shoplifting in the town and that it must be stopped. Fortunately some shops employed store detectives to help them stop the plague of female shoplifters.'

A month later, the headline read 'Epidemic of Petty Thefts'. In this case the thefts were from a vending machine and coffee stall and the culprits were six young soldiers, two of whom had been bound over for other offences. Stealing cigarettes is perhaps understandable, but taking a whole chocolate vending machine away and breaking into it is less so. Private Heaven told the court that they thought if they committed the offences they would get sent abroad which is what they wanted. The two soldiers with criminal records were sentenced to prison; the others were let off with costs and sent back to the army.

There was a wave of bike thefts towards the end of the year. In one hearing, seven boys were convicted of being involved in the theft of fifteen bicycles. Aged between 11 and 16, the boys had also stolen a dynamo and money. One boy was sent to an approved school; his father said he could not control him. The stolen bikes had to go somewhere, and in December, Bertram Pearson, a cycle dealer on King's Road, was charged with the offence of receiving a stolen cycle.

In December, 19-year-old Leslie Endicott from Meadow Road, Earley, was sent to prison for three months with hard labour for stealing a bicycle lamp. He was already on probation for stealing cigarettes, later for taking a garden frame and on another occasion for failing to obey traffic signals and riding a motor cycle with no licence, no insurance and inefficient brakes and silencer.

Car crime was common. Frank Golder of Vachel Road ran a red light on King's Road and was fined £2; Robert Price of Crowthorne caused an accident at Earley crossroads, while a 14-year-old caught driving without a licence was banned from having a licence for four years.

More serious was the theft, by persons unknown, of an attaché case from a doctor's car in Kendrick Road. Why the doctor had left his bag containing 'very dangerous drugs, including morphine and strychnine' in the car was not explained, just a note to be careful, as in the hands of inexperienced people or children the drugs could have fatal results.

There were many soldiers in the town, looked upon by the populace as guardians, men who would die to save their country. It possibly came as a shock to many readers to find out that they were not all like that. Many soldiers were charged with offences during the war, and in December five were charged during the same sitting of the Reading Police Court, all for theft of various items.

The rising crime wave was confirmed by the Chief Constable of Berkshire in his quarterly report for the three months to the end of September. It clearly showed crime was on the rise compared to a year earlier. There were 47 cases of burglary/housebreaking compared to 30; 34 cases of shop breaking compared to 25; and 'for all classes of offences 24 persons were placed under the Probation Officer and there have been 53 juvenile offenders, an increase of 22 compared with the previous year.' Just eleven people were sent for trial at the assizes, most being dealt with by the local courts. Only one sex offender was noted: Frederick Chun of Thirlmere Avenue pleaded guilty to an indecent offence.

Suicides and fatal accidents were reported. In the first months of the war they included the death by misadventure of Reginald Lipscombe who sustained a fractured skull when the brakes of his lorry failed. Private Murphy sustained fatal injuries when the car he was a passenger in skidded in the Basingstoke Road. Mrs Dewe, of Kidmore End Road, gassed herself because she was worried about the state of her health and the war; James Mowat of Wokingham was also disturbed by the war and swallowed over twenty times the lethal dose of nicotine sulphate, and Mrs Edith Emery gassed herself over worries about a public house being built near the one she owned.

Accidents on the road were such a part of life that *The Standard* ran a column: Accidents of the week. A typical round-up of the week's non-fatal accidents in the middle of October included a 5-year-old who suffered knee and foot injuries caused by a trolley bus; two 16-year-old motor cyclists were detained in hospital after an accident on Kentwood Hill; May Maslen was admitted with head injuries after being hit by a car; three members of the Patrick family were hospitalised after a car smash on the Shinfield Road and, after a five vehicle accident on the Oxford Road, only the 19-year-old motor cyclist was admitted to hospital. In November a university lecturer was knocked down by a trolley bus in Broad Street, and admitted to the Royal Berkshire Hospital. She died four hours later.

Alcohol often featured in court proceedings. Most drunks did not come easily or want to go to the station, but Harry Sowden did. A labourer of no fixed abode, he had an interesting reason for his behaviour and was glad to have been brought in. Found staggering in Bridge Street, he was abusive when told to pull himself together. He was arrested and in court told the magistrate that he had felt unwell and drunk some rum and milk and when he went 'outside he was overcome by the fresh air and did not know where he was because of the darkness. The constable did the proper thing by bringing me to the police station,' he added. Superintendent Osborne told him that he should be grateful as he might have been run over. He was fined 10s and ordered to pay 5s for the police ambulance. Frederick Fitchett of Catherine Street was fined 10s for being drunk and ordered to pay 5s for the police ambulance. He had been found helpless on the street through drink and had injured his nose. Pleading guilty, he stated he had only drunk a pint and had walked into a tramway post in the blackout.

Constable Rippington from Woodley police station had to grapple with a drunken Charles Bradbury of Winnersh. Bradbury was waving a revolver and threatening to kill someone. Fortunately the gun was not loaded. As well as being in possession of a firearm and ammunition without a licence, he had stolen a bicycle. As he was employed at Woodley aerodrome and had no previous convictions, he was fined £3, but as he had ridden the stolen bike without front or rear lights he was fined a further 15s.

Too young to drink but old enough to be in court on firearms charges: in just two months Reading Juvenile court dealt with six gun crimes with the defendants being between 11 and 14. In one case a boy was shot in the eye with a pellet. In all cases the parents were ordered to pay costs and the cases were dismissed under the Probation of Offenders Act. Juvenile crime was a common feature of the court reports. In a May sitting of the Reading magistrates, six juveniles appeared, aged between 13 and 15. Only one was girl. She was given probation for stealing a bicycle.

Gun crime was apparently in vogue because shortly after these events a man with what appeared to be a gun threatened the cleaner of a house in Bucklebury. On entering the house to demand money, he was tricked to leave and was thrown a shilling. After this he disappeared.

Among the stories of forgetfulness, mistakes and wrongdoings the papers also reported positive happenings such as weddings, wedding anniversaries and civic bravery. Ronald Broadhurst of Gas Cottages was a very lucky 7-year-old who used up his second life in October. At the age of five he had been pulled out of the Thames and two years later was rescued from the Kennet by Victor Hartwell. Anthony Martin, aged 6, a London evacuee, staying with his grandparents in Elgar Road, was not so lucky. He was found dead in the Kennet near the Berkeley Avenue Bridge.

The visit of royalty to the town was always welcome. As his father had done in the last war, King George VI visited towns and cities across the country. One of his earliest visits was to Reading. On 27 October he secretly and informally visited troops in training at Brock Barracks, described in the papers as somewhere in Berkshire. Six weeks later, Reading was visited by another VIP, the Minister of Health, Walter Elliot.

By the end of the year salvage collection and recycling were in full swing, with Scouts being heavily involved. There was money in waste and it was for a good cause. In November they cleared a cellar full of expired insurance policies and letter books dating back to 1905. Not only was their work of national importance – helping reduce the shortage of wood pulp – but it also removed from the town a potential fire danger.

Poppy Day went ahead and it was decided that in future the monies raised should benefit service personnel from any war. Over 140,000 poppies and wreaths were ordered for Reading, Sonning and Woodley. Despite the war, everything was to proceed

King George VI, like his father in the Great War, spent considerable time travelling around the country raising morale. Here he is inspecting the local Home Guard.

as normal. The only difference was that blue cornflowers, the French equivalent of the poppy, would also be sold but only in limited quantities. The day was a success with 90,000 poppies being sold and over £1,829 raised; an increase on 1938.

Although most ARP personnel were volunteers, somehow Reading was paying a weekly wage bill of £1,848; down from the peak of £2,206, but they were urgently seeking ways to cut the bill further.

It was decided that the Armistice commemoration on 11 November would be informal to avoid the danger of having a large crowd to disperse if there was an attack. Nevertheless, the Mayor, Deputy Mayor and Town Clerk walked from the Town Hall to the Forbury and placed a wreath on the memorial; a number of other official wreaths were laid alongside those from members of the public. In Reading Cemetery, Mrs Cocks of De Beauvoir Road placed flowers on the graves of the German soldiers buried there during the Great War. The vicar of St. Peter's Church in Earley hoped that people would slip into a church at 11 am that day to remember the fallen.

The next day, Sunday, 12 November, churches across the town held remembrance services. Earley went ahead with its annual parade. 'Members of the Reading and Caversham Veterans' Association, the Reading branch of the South African Wars Veterans' Association, and the Earley and East Reading branch of the British Legion assembled at Palmer Park Avenue, headed by the Spring Gardens Band, for evensong,' held in the afternoon because of blackout.

Armistice Day was not treated seriously by all in the town. Only two people placed flowers on the Caversham war memorial and around it were a group of university rowers. They were taking no notice of the importance of the day and 'were standing on the steps, leaning their cycles and scraping their shoes to rid themselves of mud, on the memorial; further, the pillar of the memorial was plastered with mud! The police had to be fetched before the students would leave.' The same sort of thing happened in Oxford.

People still enjoyed themselves. Reading's cinemas did well and people went dancing and to concerts. The Olympia in London Street was a popular venue that held, among other activities, lunchtime concerts. One highlighted was an hour of song by a Danish singer, Engel Lund, who gave a recital of international folk songs, including some from Germany. The column writer made an interesting comment: 'The Jewish race have little to rejoice about to-day, but there are many light-hearted Yiddish songs dating from less tragic times.' The programme included three Jewish songs, 'some of the most beautiful in the programme'. And at the end of November Joe Loss and his band played at the Odeon. He was followed by Tommy Trinder.

The entertainment was not just for civilians. Fred Brezin and his Reading Company of Amateurs were holding shows around the county every night for those in uniform. With a combination of song and performance he entertained the men as he had done in the Great War. For his services in the last war he had been awarded the Medaille de la Reconnaissance Française and the Medaille de la Mutalité.

Reading Art Gallery ran an exhibition of Great War cartoons by the Dutch artist Louis Raemaecker. Although they had been previously exhibited in the gallery, they were felt to be particularly appropriate at the time.

For those interested in ornithology there was the usual Reading and District Cage Bird Society event to look forward to. Exhibits came from across the south and west of England – 430 birds in total. There was obviously no shortage of bird seed yet.

Flying machines were also proving to be of increased interest. The Reading and District Model Aircraft Club was financially healthy and had more than forty members. To beat the blackout, most flying was done indoors and, just before Christmas, the club pole-flying record (a plane tied to a pole) of 37 seconds was broken.

Rather late in the year, the Fourth Arm of Defence was launched by the Chancellor of the Exchequer. This was in the form of a War Saving's campaign comprising two gilt-edged securities: a three per cent Defence Bond sold in denominations of £5 and multiples of £5, and National Savings Certificates costing 15s and worth 17s 6d in five years. The bonus was that the interest was tax-free.

During the run-up to Christmas, people were reminded of the numerous refugees in the town. The Reading Refugees Committee asked for invitations for the refugees to spend a period of time with people of their own age and preferably out of the town. They were looking to provide respite time for four young refugees, aged 9 to 24 (two Catholics and two non-observant Jews), at least two of whom had a mother in a concentration camp. They also needed winter clothes for refugees from Nazi Germany and bicycles for the men. All refugees were welcomed at the Friends' House on Thursdays from 4 pm to 9.30 pm.

Many of the evacuees were no doubt looking forward to Christmas at home but the government felt differently. They felt they should stay in safer areas and the papers agreed, telling readers 'there are times when it is necessary, as it were, to be cruel only to be kind.' There were half a million children away from their homes, most of whom wanted to go home.

Stating the obvious, *The Standard* told readers that the coming Christmas would 'in many respects be different from that of other years'. It asked though, as far as possible, that people should maintain the old spirit, particularly for the children who were assured that Santa Claus would make a special effort to ensure his benevolence was generously rationed.

McIlroy's department store was not going to let the children down or miss the chance to increase turnover. Once again they boasted Father Christmas in store. They were able to use the same man again; indeed it was his thirteenth Christmas for McIlroy's. It was an impressive entrance and display for the several thousand children gathered at the store. Santa came down a chimney and stepped out of a giant fireplace. 'The chimney was in the balcony of the shop, and the ground floor and showroom were so full that police were needed to control the crowds. Father Christmas was accompanied by fairies and snow-maidens, and two trumpeters heralded his arrival.' Santa was greeted by the Mayor, Councillor W. McIlroy, and then went down to his house in the basement, followed by many children who wanted to receive presents, slightly different from today. Leading to his house was a fairy tale and woodland scene that included the babes in the wood sleeping under leaves, with rabbits, owls and woodland creatures moving around them. Over the weekend McIlroy's sold more toys than in the corresponding period in 1938.

Not all the children or parents were pleased with the visit to Santa. One mother commented that the trip to see Father Christmas was something her 5-year-old son, with sixpence clutched in his hand, had waited for. At the end of his visit he had scarcely glimpsed Santa and came away with a writing pad. The child was in tears, and the writer wondered why, if it had to be so crassly commercialised, no imagination had been used to provide something better.

'Christmas Parcels for the Blind' was the heading to an appeal from the County Blind Society. They were appealing for donations to help blind people make ends meet in a time of rising prices and buy them parcels of Christmas fare.

As in the Great War, there was a Christmas pudding appeal for soldiers at the front. Any pudding sent had to be in a non-breakable container which could be steam heated in a short time. Once again they asked for the usual items of clothing.

Not wanting to put a damper on any Christmas festivities, the Ministry of Health issued 'a memorandum on the subject of influenza'. Although there was no epidemic at the time, it emphasised that it was always present and that its effects in wartime might be serious, echoing the Great War pandemic. It recommended cod liver oil and a morning and night gargle.

Winter brought frozen pipes: inconvenient, and plumbers were hard to find. People were told to prepare for the frosts. *The Standard* provided tips: for insulation, sandbags loosely filled with sawdust or shavings, newspaper, tarpaulins and roofing felt. Blankets and hay were suitable for lagging pipes.

Christmas did nothing to reduce accidents. The 8 December 'Accidents of the Week' column featured three pedestrians knocked down by cars and a cycling accident. Two of the car accidents resulted in leg injuries, one in abrasions, and the cyclist who skidded had abrasions and shock.

Neither did it bring good cheer for men between 20 and 22. This age group was called up under the National Service (Armed Forces) Act on 16 December.

However, there was good news for consumers: there was no food shortage in Reading and food shops would open on Boxing Day morning and then close for the usual half-day. Other shops stayed closed to give workers as long a break as possible. While most were at home on Boxing Day morning, Reading's refuse collectors were out, not to collect the bins but to receive their Christmas tip.

Just before Christmas people were informed about how well their trams and buses were doing, although not everybody agreed, with full buses passing waiting crowds and rushes to board buses. The suggestion was to form orderly queues. The good news was that some fares had gone down. Although the

Another job taken over by women was bus conductor. This conductress is working for the Thames Valley Traction bus company.

accounts report was mainly about pre-war performance, the buses showed a massive increase in profits from £1,892 (same half-year in 1938) to £5,578, which would help keep down any rate rise.

Christmas 1939 saw the first performance of Cinderella at the Palace. It had a familiar cast, plus a number of speciality acts such as the Flying Potter in 'aerial bounce', Sylvia Dale's Ten

Wonderful Youngsters and Hyda Smith's Fifteen Adderley High Steppers; it must have been a busy stage. *Jamaica Inn* was on at the Central in Friar Street and at the Regal in Caversham was *Cheer, Boys, Cheer*. On Boxing Night Teddy Hale's Band was providing the dance music at the Olympia. For those fancying a flutter, there were races at Cheltenham on 28 December and Newbury on 29 and 30 December with trains from Reading to the racecourse. Interestingly, the trains would only be using first and third class carriages; a reflection on those expected to travel to the races?

Another wartime Christmas tradition was appeals for funds. The Mayor wanted money to provide festivities for the evacuated children at the schools they were sharing with local children, and the County Blind Society was raising money to provide Christmas hampers.

Christmas is a time of good cheer. A supper and social at the White Hart Hotel was held for head and instructor wardens of the local ARP, which meant stocking the drinks cabinet, and, celebrating their 110th Christmas in business, Butler & Sons of Chatham Street advised customers to shop early to buy at pre-budget prices. Open from 10 am to 8 pm, they were offering spirits and imported wines from Europe and the Empire plus some British products 'all of good alcoholic strength': cowslip, elder, orange and raisin, all at 2s a bottle, or a 1933 Bordeaux at 2s 2d.

Always benevolent, Huntley & Palmers Recreation Club gave their annual Christmas party for children of members. It was four hours long and included a ventriloquist, Punch & Judy and a film show. This was followed by tea, with lucky ticket holders receiving presents and, to finish the event, they visited Santa in a gaily decorated cave. Each was given a bag containing sweets, an apple, banana, and an orange.

Evacuated children were also treated to a party. A joint committee from the LCC and local Head Teachers under the chairmanship of the Mayor held parties for the thousands of London children and also provided them with film shows, presents and entertainment in the form of the Czech Refugees' concert party, conjurors and comedians. It was no mean task to entertain 17,000 evacuees and Reading schoolchildren. The entertainments were held in schools and halls across Reading. The simplest part was giving out a blue and white New Year card to each child bearing the good wishes of the Mayor.

Some 180 evacuated children from Battersea who were being taught at Earley St. Peter's School were entertained to tea in the church hall. The money for the tea and party were raised by the Earley pupils.

The elderly, the sick and the poor were remembered. Over 1,000 food parcels were delivered to the Old Age Pensioners of the town by the Reading Philanthropic Institution. 'Included in the food parcels was a joint of meat, sausages, dripping, rice, biscuits, cake, Oxo cubes, Quaker Oats, tea, sugar, milk, honey, peas, flour, oranges, sweets and a few crackers.'

All over the town children performed in nativity plays. Typical was that given at the Cumberland Road Methodist Church Hall. What was different was that it was given by the children from Stonehouse Street Junior Mixed School of Clapham High Street, evacuated to Reading and billeted in the Cemetery Junction area, to their foster parents.

On the front page of the 22 December edition of *The Standard* was an important notice for shoppers although it was actually aimed at local shops. 'The Reading Chamber of Commerce recommends its members who sell non-perishable goods to remain closed from Saturday night to Thursday, 28/12/39, usual opening time. All others, including offices, were to re-open on Wednesday, 27/12/39, usual opening time.' Fortunately, food shops could open.

There was also to be a change to blackout rules to help Christmas shopping. A measure of lighting was to be allowed experimentally on stalls in the streets and in open markets during blackout hours up to the hour fixed for the closing of shops in Reading. This was to help Christmas shopping. It was strictly controlled: the stall had to be lightproof except at one end, any light could be not brighter than needed to see the goods, nor shed light outside the stall and had to be extinguishable quickly in the event of an air raid.

Any hook was used to sell goods in peacetime: war provided a new angle. A pre-Christmas pitch from Jacksons to be the shop to buy from for those at the front.

On the first Christmas of the war, rather less eventful than anticipated, the vicar of Sonning summed up the feelings of many: 'Never did we need more the great Christmas message of Peace and Good-will.' The columnist Karandash wrote that 'Christmas must not be looked upon as a time of gloom. All should radiate good cheer in the confidence that in the end our good cause must prevail...And so, at this Christmastide of 1939, we should all – if for no other reason, then do it for the sake of the children – keep up the old rejoicings, the old exchanges of greetings, the old festivities, the family gatherings, the Christmas cheer. These are symbolic of the home fires burning and they must be kept burning.'

Come what may, there was always beer. One advert wished readers 'The Season's Compliments' and went on to expound the importance of the beverage: 'There are some things the war can't stop. It can't stop Christmas cheerfulness. It can't stop the ring of laughter, and kindly greetings. It can't stop our preference for the glass of beer which makes for cheeriness and good fellowship. In sad days and glad days beer has played its part… It has heartened us in the last few months…It will keep you in good form, sharpen up your appetite, make you hearty and healthy…beer is best. It will help to make – a happy Christmas.'

Coincidentally on the same page was a report about H & G Simonds, a local brewer. They were celebrating 70 million bottles of beer sold and a net profit of £221,593, no doubt drinking to another bumper year in 1940, as evidenced by the gossip column. 'There were many Old King Coles about, their ruddy countenance reflecting the merry mood of the moment… unanimous in calling for their glasses.'

Naturally with all that good cheer there were cases of over indulgence. Ernest Wells, with eleven previous convictions for the same offence, was fined 10s and ordered to pay 5s for the police van for being drunk outside the Abbey Hall at 3.30 pm. Richard Heffernan was charged with being drunk and disorderly in London Street at 10.45 am and fined 10s or the alternative of seven days. And Frederick East from Oxford was arrested for being drunk in Station Approach. He was well known to the police, having 22 previous convictions over 28 years for drunkenness, assault on the police and larceny.

Until September the men of the Star & Garter Home in Richmond had received a daily half-pint beer ration because it did them good. Since the war they had been on a Sunday ration until just before Christmas when donations made it possible for them to have it three times a week. Donations were wanted to restore the seven days a week distribution.

Some did not need alcohol to be disorderly. On the Saturday before Christmas, two Reading police officers were assaulted when fourteen Irishmen and three soldiers were involved in a fight in the Cambridge Café in Hosier Street. Only one man was taken to court, 20-year-old Christopher Gallagher who was sentenced to one month for assaulting DC Allen, one month for assaulting PS Blundell and fourteen days for fighting, the terms to run consecutively.

Perhaps the size of the good wishes from *The Standard* was a comment on the war. In just a column inch, it wished its readers 'A Happy Christmas'. Appropriately, the last issue before the festival during which many would overeat carried its usual advert for Milk of Magnesia tablets. They would help the user 'avoid flatulence and pain after meals'.

Churches were busy over the Christmas period but the blackout reduced the number of attendees. This was because there were no midnight services.

The Standard told readers that the year drawing to its close had been born with gloomy foreboding and was ending in an atmosphere of restlessness. It then condemned the Munich Pact as a betrayal worse than that of Judas Iscariot and reminded readers of the horrors of the Nazi regime. Then, bolstering spirits, it wrote that although the future was uncertain 'we have faith in the justice of the cause for the vindication of which we have taken up arms…to win peace.'

The Mayor, Councillor McIlroy, wished everyone a happy New Year and not only to those who were resident. He remembered that many were serving and sent the greeting to 'men in the Royal Navy facing the perils of the seas; men in the army waiting for the command "Stand to!"; men of the Royal Air Force maintaining their heroic and constant watchfulness'. And, not forgetting the auxiliary women's services, he hoped that everyone would find happiness through the satisfaction of duty and service in these days of waiting and difficulty. In a similar vein, Councillor Hewitt told readers to 'keep calm and be confident that the British Empire and France together will make sure of victory.' He also urged the purchase of bonds and certificates.

There was an appeal to dog owners. The secretary of Our Dumb Friends' League asked owners who could not afford to renew their dog licence (in one sitting of the Borough Police

Court in August, twenty-two people were fined for not renewing their licence), not to throw them out on the street, but take them to a dispensary or shelter where they would be looked after. In conjunction with the PDSA, they were prepared, upon proof of inability to pay, to purchase the licence for the owner. Strangely, although the dog pound was generally full of strays, many people offered to take in dog refugees from bombed areas rather than house local dogs.

An appeal of a different sort was made by the Lord Lieutenant. The Commander-in-Chief of Aldershot Command wanted Reading to open its doors to the large number of Dominion troops who were about to be based in the area. He wanted offers of accommodation and meals for weekends, visits to places of interest and the chance to play sports like golf or tennis.

The Chief Constable of Reading drew attention to regulations governing noise. Sirens, engine whistles, and instruments of a similar description were not allowed to be sounded. However, sirens would be allowed once a month in the New Year. The air raid sirens would be tested in Reading at 1 pm on the first Sunday of every month.

Later, in 1940, the Minister of Home Security announced that 'to defeat enemy attempts to dislocate civil life and particularly war industrial production, workers are…encouraged to stay at work after air raid warning sirens have sounded until it is clear that an enemy attack is imminent.' Not long after this advice Alderman Bale told the town that everyone should 'take cover when the sirens sound' and certainly not stand and gaze up at what was happening as this would cause crowds to form and increase casualties. Neither should they stand in their doorway and watch.

One soldier got into trouble for seeing in the New Year nine hours early. French-Canadian Angus Daigle, who pleaded not guilty, was fined for being drunk and disorderly outside Marks & Spencer in the middle of the afternoon.

The Ministry of Food announced that from 8 January rationing was to be extended to sugar. Each person would be entitled to ¾ lb a week. Meat rationing would follow. The papers would provide tips on economy.

Even with such uncertainty about the future people still got married. This is the wedding of Sub-Lieutenant Leonard D. Habbitts, RNVR, and Miss Beryl Jennings at St. Luke's church on Erleigh Road. They both survived the war.

CHAPTER TWO

1940

After a subdued Christmas, there was no reason not to see in the New Year, with the hope that it would be the last year of the war. In Sonning, the locals went to a dance. 'In these difficult days, we not only need to have our lives brightened by happy social gatherings, but also to have our wills strengthened by the grace

As men were called up, their places were taken by women. This is a scene in a local factory, probably Miles Aircraft as the engine appears to be one for an aircraft.

of God for all that may be in front of us during the coming year, which we hope and pray may be a year that brings with it true and lasting peace,' declared the vicar.

But many were wondering what would happen if Reading was bombed. Fortunately 'plans for accommodation and feeding in the event of an air raid' were in hand. It was complicated but it was believed there would be sufficient food and sufficient buildings available for those bombed out: St. Barnabas's Hall, Whitley, would accommodate 50 persons; Wesley Hall, 100; St. Saviour's Hall, 100; London Street Chapel, 100; and Trinity Congregational Institute, 100.

Accidents continued to happen. Just days into the New Year, Nancy Hughes was detained in hospital with head injuries when the car she was a passenger in collided with a trolley bus standard. The same day, Arthur Gibson had a motor bike accident and Ralph King suffered head and shoulder injuries in a traffic accident near Loddon Bridge. The next day Winifred Nicholls skidded on her cycle and Albert Reynolds suffered head injuries in a traffic accident near Earley Station. In May, after a darts match, William Lee drove from the Borough Arms along Temple Place, Coley. He missed his way and backed the car into the Kennet. Fortunately the car landed upright and he and his two passengers managed to escape through the sun roof and by opening the car doors. The water was up to the roof. They were rescued by boat.

The year was only two days old when a robbery took place. For the second time in less than nine months, Frame's clothing manufacturing premises in Greyfriars Road was broken into. Valued at about £150, the haul included 40 raincoats and 120 suits. In a different raid, thieves stole cigarettes and tobacco from a wholesale supplies company. The next day, Burdis Redford was charged with robbery and violence. He had robbed Gladys Smith of the Red Cow public house, using violence against her. It took nearly a year, but on 5 January, Henry North of 387, London Road, appeared in court for embezzling and stealing £60 from Goring Parish Council.

Each week there were reports of wrongdoing. Typical stories across the year were: two boys who stole two syphons tried to sell them to their owners; two boys were fined for maliciously cutting two trees; and two boys were summoned for throwing stones at a street lamp. A 13-year-old boy, who had appeared before the bench only the week before, was sent to an Approved School for stealing a carton of liquorice valued at 6s. Edward Rawling of Hazel Crescent took four blank cheques. William Catlin was fined £1 for stealing twigs from a private wood. One 11-year-old boy, an inveterate liar who was out of control but no trouble at school, was a long-term truant and branded as sly and of little ability. He asked to be sent to a remand home. His parents got rid of their problem for just 2s 6d a week maintenance while he was at the school. A problem boy from Winnersh, told that he needed a thorough flogging for stealing 4s 2d, was made to pay the money back and bound over for two years. Colonel Barker the magistrate felt that flogging would stop juvenile crime which he said was getting dreadful. The anonymous letter writer 'Rambler' agreed: 'Spare the rod and spoil the child.'

The big heist was the theft of 22,000 cigarettes from the Buckland Road Co-op store by three local lads. Two brothers, Ernest of Brixham Road and Leslie Anderson of Torrington Road, with their friend Thomas Grigg of Meavy Gardens, had climbed onto a flat roof and entered the shop through a window. The brothers were bound over for twelve months while Griggs, who had been to borstal, was given twelve months' hard labour. A chef, Albert Foster of Watlington Street, was bound over for buying some of the stolen cigarettes.

In April a new form of burglary was reported in Beresford Road. While householders slept, a group of four men went from house to house taking money from handbags and purses. They then drove away.

Not all the criminals were local or male. Mary, an evacuee mother from Putney, was bound over for twelve months for stealing various household items from the house in Tilehurst where she was living.

Lillian Archer of Basingstoke Road was fined 5s for striking Adelaide Hornblower on the head with a glass jar. In Earley, a Dartmoor escapee was sighted but not apprehended.

Probably the most common crime was still breach of blackout. The Reverend Tyres was fined 10s for showing an unobscured light from the church vestry in Kidmore End Church. Mrs Evans of Rupert Street was also fined 10s for displaying an unobscured light at her shop. By early August, in eleven months of war, Reading Police Court had dealt with 500 blackout offences. Possibly the most serious punishment, a month's imprisonment, was given to a man who struck a match in the street during the blackout. On being rebuked he lit another match and was arrested.

Although not a major crime, milk dilution was illegal. In just one week, two separate farms were fined for adding water to the milk. And two 13-year-old boys were caught stealing and drinking milk.

There was domestic crime. Mrs Richardson was convicted of assaulting her husband, from whom she was separated, while he was enjoying a drink in a public house in Friar Street.

According to the Chief Constable of Berkshire there had been a considerable increase in crime over the year from Easter 1939. Unlike the local papers, he did not blame juveniles for it as there had been a drop in such cases. However, 16 evacuees had been responsible for 16 indictable offences. In total nearly 4,000 crimes had been committed in Berkshire of which just 47 had been sent to trial. However, in his first report for 1940 he reported that crime had fallen.

The same could not be said for the death toll on the roads. Compared to the same time in 1939 when eight had been killed, in 1940 it was 11, with three deaths a result of the blackout. The number of injured had fallen.

Although opposed, hunting continued. Meetings continued to be held every week. By the end of the season in May 1940 they felt proud to have killed more than the average number of foxes even though they had been unable to hunt for seventeen days.

People continued to drive while intoxicated. Riding School proprietor James Black of Earley was fined £3, ordered to pay £2 7s costs and his licence was endorsed for colliding with a cycle being pushed by the side of the road. Admitting to drinking four pints, he thought however that he was not under the influence of alcohol.

Stories of over-indulgence were regularly reported: a drunken Canadian who wanted to fight, and William Hickey of Staverton Road who was found helpless across a car bonnet. He had a good excuse and was ashamed of his behaviour. Not being a habitual drinker and having suffered from sunstroke twice, he told the Bench that drink made him physically and mentally helpless and that he hadn't meant to drink the bottle in Broad Street, but he met a friend. Full of sympathy the Bench fined him 10s for being drunk. During the year only 51 people (30 strangers to the town) had been prosecuted for drunkenness, of which 47 were convicted. Ronald Duff was luckier. Appearing in the dock on crutches, he had lost a leg in the Great War. He blamed his drunkenness on a lapse because he had met friends he had not seen for years and after months of temperance the wine upset him. His case was dismissed.

Perhaps such cases were not a true reflection of the town. During the first four months of the war Reading had officially become, even with the massive increase of inhabitants, a more sober place. In 1937 it had topped the sobriety list, falling in 1938 to 8th place and in 1939 rising to be 7th. There was a public house to every 422 members of the population.

In February, a Reading club was raided. The Dukes Club in King Street was said to be the resort of criminals and loose women but this was naturally denied by the joint proprietor, Sidney Barker. Showing how seriously he took his position as secretary of a member-only club, the visitor's book was used in evidence. Among the guests had been Jean Harlow, dead since 1937, Donald Duck, Popeye and Tom Mix. He was fined £40 for allowing the sale of alcohol on four separate occasions before Christmas 1939 in contravention of the Licensing Consolidation Act, 1910.

Reading Fire Brigade was called out to two fires within twenty-four hours. The first at 28, Shepherd's Lane was timber burning under a bedroom floor near a fireplace; a simple solution was to remove the fireplace. In Castle Street, a suite of furniture was found on fire in the basement; the fire was put out before it could spread. Running parallel with the local brigade was the

Auxiliary Fire Service. They were volunteers with other regular employment and were liable to call-up. The problem was that they were needed at home and in the forces and, if they asked for deferment from military service, they were concerned they would be seen as conscientious objectors.

Reading celebrated the achievements of one of its sons. The submarine HMS *Sunfish*, commanded by the appropriately named Lieutenant Commander Jack Slaughter, sank four German ships during the Norwegian campaign. Before joining the navy he had lived in Alexandra Road with his mother.

Later in the year, Bearwood School welcomed back an ex-pupil, Lieutenant Commander Stannard. He had been awarded the Victoria Cross for his heroism in the Norwegian Campaign.

The period from September 1939 to May 1940 was known as the Phoney War because the army was holding static defensive positions in France. Consequently local casualties were limited. The first Reading man to be killed in action in 1940 was Thomas Edward Tegg of Caversham, a petty officer aboard HMS *Grenville,* which was mined in the Thames Estuary on 19 January. He had served throughout the Great War and already completed his twenty-one years' service before re-enlisting. Two days later Leading Signalman Eric Pragnell of South Street, Caversham, died when HMS *Exmouth* was sunk with all hands. Three weeks after the death of PO Tegg, the residents of another house in the same street learned that Able Seaman Still, a naval reservist, had been lost when the destroyer HMS *Daring* had been torpedoed.

One lucky Reading sailor was Petty Officer Coxswain Ernest Redgate. On 9 January the submarine *Starfish* was sunk in the Heligoland Bight, amazingly with no loss. After being missing a month, a card arrived from Germany informing his family he was safe.

Before the German invasion of Holland, most deaths were of sailors and airmen. In April, two men serving on HMS *Glowworm* were killed at sea: Able Seaman Cyril Taylor of Circuit Lane was close to retirement and 27-year-old Chief Petty Officer Leonard Harman of Birch Avenue was an only son.

With the fighting before Dunkirk, the roll of honour began to include soldiers such as Second Lieutenant Laidlaw of Pitts Lane, Private Hamblin of Providence Place and Lance Bombardier Tranter of Granby Gardens. The paper stated he had been killed at Dunkirk, but he is buried in the Henley Road Cemetery. All three were killed in France.

Not all military deaths were caused by the enemy. Boy soldier Stanley Hayter died in the Royal Berks on 8 June; he was too young to serve abroad. Another boy soldier, Desmond Hall, aged 15½, was accidentally shot in the neck while in the barracks. The coroner returned a verdict of Death by Misadventure. Three weeks after joining the RAF, Norman Darby was accidentally shot while training and died.

There were also happy stories about service personnel. In the confusion after Dunkirk, many were listed as missing and continued to be missing until confirmed as dead. Some of the missing were confirmed as PoWs many months later, like Sapper Ronald 'Tom' White, of 108 Castle Street; he had joined the Royal Engineers just months before the war.

The minimum age for ship service in the Royal Navy was 18 but many boys joined at 14 or even younger. They could only fulfil roles on land until they were old enough. This is Major Collett, the son of a Reading police officer who had joined at 13½ and when war broke out he joined the Merchant Navy at the age of 14; they allowed youngsters to serve aboard because it was simply civilian employment. He looked older, as this photo shows.

Normal home life also brought tragedy. In the space of a weekend in February, Mr and Mrs Sherwood, of Wilton Road, lost all their three children to a serious illness. A week later, Mr and Mrs Liddon of Mortlake lost their only child, Edwin. He was an evacuee living in Reading. Although the boy was ill for nearly two weeks his parents were not informed. Another sad loss both to the families and the war effort was the joint suicide of Alan Borland of Earley, a married man and father of three small children, and Pamela Tomlinson who was lodging in Earley. They had worked together at Woodley Aerodrome.

Another loss was one of Reading's oldest inhabitants, Mrs Rhoda Davis of Peppard Road, who died in her 94th year. As a child during the Crimean War she had made bandages for the troops. She had lost her only son during the Great War and was survived by four daughters.

In July Reading's oldest woman, Bridget Tovey, celebrated her 100th birthday. She was still busy making comforts for the troops.

Unlike in the Great War, initially there were no mass marches to aid recruiting. However, later in the year the authorities, realising the part women could play in the armed forces, did start recruitment marches through the town. Recruiting meetings were also held in the Town Hall with posters prominently displayed in cinemas. The first major recruiting drive was for the Women's Land Army. Among those who answered the call were ballet dancers, beauty specialists, mannequins, typists and art students.

The most essential of these were the typists. The military machine relied on written orders and there were few men with that particular skill. With hundreds of positions available, the Berkshire School of Shorthand in Blagrave Street was running courses 'to assist in the successful prosecution of the war'. By the end of the year the demand was for women to work in the engineering industry where they could earn good wages.

When insufficient women came forward there was always the schoolboy. The chance was to be offered to Reading boys who had just left school and those returning in the autumn to work at summer 'holiday farming' camps. Accommodation was to be in

Like their male counterparts, members of the ATS were also paraded and inspected. In this case the 11th Berkshire Company is being inspected by the County Commandant and the Company Commander while a junior commander is seen adjusting the cap of one of the members.

barns or under canvas, boys to provide their own bedding and clothing. It was not slave labour: boys under 16 would receive 5d an hour, 6d an hour for those over 16.

When the Minister of Agriculture released figures that showed how much food had previously been imported, it was obvious that the increase of 300,000 allotments since the war began would not be enough. Three figures summed up how much food the country would be short: in 1939 the country had imported five million cwt of onions, 211,000 cwt of lettuce and 200,000 cwt of broccoli and cauliflower. Digging for Victory involved new enemies: insects were dealt with by a range of toxic insecticides and birds, no longer the beautiful singing creatures prized in gardens, ate flowering buds, took seeds from the ground and consumed fresh fruits and vegetables.

Although there had been issues about the bill for ARP, more volunteers were asked for as well as people to join the Auxiliary

Fire Service. With regard to the shortage of gas masks, Civil Defence was able to report that fifty per cent of the gas masks needed for young children had now been distributed with the remainder on the way. However, at the same time, Wokingham was able to supply them to anyone who required them.

From 8 April, any damage to or loss of a civilian respirator, except through enemy action, would be charged to the owner. A lost mask would cost 2s 6d, a lost or damaged face piece 1s 6d, a container 1s, a carton 2d. A child's respirator was more expensive: complete loss with carton was 3s 6d, a lost or damaged face piece 2s 6d. A baby's anti-gas helmet was even more expensive. Complete replacement including carton was 25s. Householders were told to expect a visit from wardens. They were asked to have their respirators ready for inspection – a strange request considering that everyone was supposed to carry them at all times.

Regardless of the war, the January sales were something to look forward to. In a large advert, the Reading Co-operative Society not only wished its members and friends a 'Bright and Prosperous New Year' but reminded them of the 'Great Winter Sale' starting on the 11th. In the summer there were also sales, not always to get rid of older stock. Some stock was bought from shops going bankrupt or that had been bombed out. The Mystery Man, a well-known Lambeth tradesman, specialised in bombed salvaged stocks, which were mostly damaged by dust and water, in his St. Mary's Butts store.

In the case of Wellsteeds in Broad Street, their 4 July sale was because they were closing down another store – Bobby's of Cliftonville; and in London Street, Lewis & Hyland were clearing £20,000 of evacuation stock. Leon's department store in Broad Street was simply having a sale. A few weeks later Wellsteeds offered even more bargains as they were closing down their Folkestone store as well. In December Lewis & Hyland in London Street were clearing stocks from their Folkestone and Ramsgate stores in time for Christmas. They were offering fur coats at pre-war prices. Who could resist a 'Chinese Cat Coat' at 17 guineas or a seal and beaver Coney coat at just 6 guineas?

For those without the money for a new fur coat, there was always remodelling to the latest style undertaken at Furmax Ltd in West Street.

Coming in with the new year was food rationing. The procedure was the same as in the previous war: shoppers registered with a licensed food retailer and exchanged money and coupons for the required goods. There were punishments for what before the war had been considered a sensible thing to do, stockpiling, now seen as hoarding.

The Ministry of Food explained why rationing was necessary: half of Britain's meat supplies and most of its butter and sugar were purchased from abroad. Rationing would prevent the waste of food, increase the war effort by reducing shipping, divide supplies equally and stop uncertainty and queues. 'Your ration book is your passport to easy purchasing of bacon & ham, butter and sugar.' On 8 January, rationing began for bacon, butter and sugar. It was relatively easy to make the butter ration go further: add an equal amount of margarine (not rationed) and a small quantity of milk and beat until mixed. After July, when all cooking fats were rationed, people could no longer stretch their butter ration with margarine.

The implementation of rationing made it essential that traders gave correct weights. Whether intentional or not, if false weights were discovered, the seller was prosecuted. A typical example was that of Baylis & Co, grocers, who were summoned on four counts of selling food and making misrepresentations calculated to mislead the purchaser as to the weight. They were prosecuted for selling ¾ lb of bacon 8½ drams underweight, ½ lb of cheese 7½ drams short, ¾ lb butter 2¾ drams underweight and 1 lb bacon 6 ¾ drams short. Found guilty, they were fined £6.

While rationing meant fair shares, it required considerable ingenuity to stop meals becoming tasteless and monotonous. To help, the government produced food pamphlets and cookery books as well as taking out space in the papers to inform readers. By the middle of the year, Reading housewives were being invited to demonstrations of wartime cookery at the Electricity Service Centre in Gun Street, hosted by the Wessex Electricity Company.

The closing date to register for meat coupons was 8 January. To control the slaughter of fatstock and the nation's meat supply the Ministry of Food, from 15 January, became the sole buyer, at fixed prices so farmers had a guaranteed market. However, meat rationing did not begin until 11 March when an adult could buy 1s 10d worth a week with coupons. For the better off, poultry and game were not rationed and, for those on more slender budgets, no coupons were required for liver, kidney, tripe, heart and oxtail. Sausages, meat pies and galantines containing not more than fifty per cent meat were also not rationed.

For many, tea rationing was the most difficult to deal with. The weekly allowance was a meagre 2 ounces (56 grams), but it could be bought in bulk as long as the purchaser had the coupons, and unlike other rationed foodstuffs did not require the purchaser to register with a shop to purchase it.

To supplement rations and provide food for the pigs, children became scavengers. During autumn they would pick blackberries for jam and pies, collect acorns to help feed the pigs and rosehips to make into vitamin-rich syrup for children. Another way of making food last was canning. In the autumn a canning school was run at Reading Cricket Club. In two days the ladies of the Earley WI produced 334 cans of fruit. A year later they had bought their own canning machine.

Not long after the introduction of meat rationing, because of the numbers suddenly keeping pigs, pork was taken off the points system and was no longer classed as meat. Bacon, however, was still in short supply.

People were encouraged to keep chickens. They were an economic supplement for the family, providing eggs and meat and could be fed on kitchen scraps. The emphasis was on chickens, not cockerels, because in the confines of a back yard they would wake people before daybreak.

Poaching – trespassing in search of game – was another way to supplement rations. Thomas Grigg of Meavy Gardens, who had previous form and had been in reform school and borstal, was fined just £1 because he had been called up by the navy. His offence was the possession of a ferret, several nets and three rabbits taken on private land in Shinfield.

Digging for Victory meant looking after an allotment or digging up the back garden to grow vegetables. To encourage the best use of an allotment, judged by the local Horticultural Panel, the Mayor offered 6 silver and 12 bronze medals, 50 certificates of merit and 50 awards of merit.

It was still possible to provide children with a treat. In January, provided by subscriptions from London and Reading, the children of the town and the evacuee children mixed when 'a jolly entertainment was given and afterwards each child received a packet of sweets, an orange and a card, the latter a gift from the Mayor of Reading'.

There were still shortages. A shortage of coal in the winter of 1940 caused the closing of Reading schools for several days. The deficiency was due to a shortage not of coal but of transport in the form of horse and motor drivers; it was so severe that women were recruited. With deliveries limited to 2cwt per house, Reading was better off than some other areas.

The coal shortage meant that people stole wood to keep warm. William White of Bramble Crescent pleaded guilty to stealing a tree trunk. The case was dismissed on payment of 15s.

Due to the severe cold the Waterworks Department dealt with 32 mains and 58 service pipes that burst in the public highway, and answered 704 calls about burst pipes, leakages, and defective stopcocks in private premises. Seventy-two visits were made to premises reported to be frozen up. To cope with frozen service pipes on the Wokingham Road, Whiteknights Road, all over Earley, Southampton Street, Berkeley Avenue, Bath Road, Kentwood Estate, Oxford Road, Bridge Street, Caroline Street and Tilehurst, a twice-daily service was provided by tanks and stand-pipes.

For those living in the countryside, the shortage of coal was less of a problem. The no-longer-needed pram now found a new use; it was ideal for collecting firewood.

The situation did not improve until mid-April and even then there was insufficient coal for the town. Although the Mayor announced that householders could purchase up to five cwt a fortnight, he added that there were still problems getting the coal delivered. However, the situation would improve later in the month because two extra trains of coal were expected. The Co-op advised householders to buy as much coal as they could to store for the coming winter. But there would be no summer price reduction. They also advised customers to maintain their stocks of canned food in case of emergency.

To stop traders marking up prices the government introduced the Prices of Goods Act. It hoped to check the vicious spiral caused by continuously rising prices alternating with consequent wage rises. The Price Regulation Committee's headquarters was in the town. It was responsible for dealing with price complaints; every product was to be compared to its price on 21 August 1939; more expensive items were not regulated. The first prosecution was in March. Messrs Frank Gale and Son, radio and cycle specialists of Friar Street, were summoned for unlawfully selling price-regulated batteries above the permitted price. As a respectable and well-established company, the case was dismissed under the Probation of Offenders Act on payment of £4 13s costs.

Despite petrol rationing, there was still a demand for new cars, and the government wanted car production for home and export to continue. Ford announced a new car designed for wartime conditions, the Anglia. It was an advance on previous ideas of taste and comfort. It was priced between £126 and £136 and was available at Gowrings. In a letter to the paper, A MOTOR TRADER told readers to keep their road wheels turning and refuse to be intimidated. For those with a car, it was best just to pay the new horsepower tax and not lay up the car for the duration. The reasons were simple. If an owner managed without a car for a period of time, why would the government give them petrol coupons if they wanted to reuse it and, secondly, did they really want to rely on the vagaries of public transport, especially if the area was bombed?

Rats were a problem, with some areas, Whitley for example, being severely infested. Manor Farm council tip was especially infested. There refuse was merely covered with a thin layer of soil, which did nothing to stop the rats scavenging. From there they spread out across the area. Why did they not simply incinerate the refuse and sell the scraps, asked a disgruntled ratepayer and allotment holder. Gardeners were upset because the rats were eating their peas and beans and digging up their potatoes.

The cold weather helped spread disease. During the early months of the year there were outbreaks of measles, whooping cough, mumps and chicken pox. Scarlet fever was also common.

Illness affected the buses. During the second week of February, seventy members of the transport department were on the sick list. Mrs Cusden, a Labour Councillor, suggested employing women as conductors because of the shortage of men, an idea quickly rejected by Councillor Palmer who said the Transport Committee felt it was undesirable to employ women.

Cold weather did not stop the Reading Pigeon Show but it did reduce the number of entries. In the Great War, keeping pigeons was strictly controlled under the Defence of the Realm Act, but in 1940 it was not seen to be necessary.

Early dark nights, cold weather and the blackout made waste-paper collection difficult. Zealots complained about using waste paper to light fires. Many families were using paper ringlets rather than scarce wood and it was difficult to see any realistic alternative. One suggestion was using dried orange and grapefruit peel.

More paper could have been saved if every council took salvage seriously. Gladys Holmes of 9 Palmerstone Road, Earley, complained about Wokingham Council's bin men. Although she put newspapers and magazines on the top of her bin for recycling, they were thrown in the refuse cart and covered with other rubbish. Bradfield Council took it more seriously, leafleting homes and using posters to encourage saving all forms of salvage.

Reading was not salvaging enough. The town was mentioned in the Commons by Minister of Supply Leslie Burgin as being a backward town for salvage collection. Defending the town, the Borough Surveyor said they collected the paper on a commercial

Ophelia Snodkins loved to ride
On the crown of the road instead of the side.
No signal she gave as she swerved to the right,
So a sprightly young life met its end that night.
Let Ophelia's ghost be a warning to you
If you wish to live to a hundred and two.

LOOK OUT IN THE BLACKOUT,

THE
THAMES • VALLEY
TRACTION COMPANY, LIMITED.

In order to combat deaths during the blackout, the papers carried stories about the demise of those who were not careful.

Aluminium was used in aircraft bodies and every attempt was made to recycle as much as possible. This is Mr E. Hillier, the official collector for Woodley, calling on a resident.

basis and this was not included in the returns. His concern was that the public, ignoring the posters, simply threw the paper into bins, stopping its collection.

However Scrap Iron Week in July was so successful it received a message of congratulations from the Director of Scrap Supplies. In three days, 240 tons were collected. The scrap collected by the refuse men included a parrot cage, toy scooters, mowers, dustbins, toy motor cars and even a complete car. The most common scrap was bedsteads.

Also given for smelting were the railings of Coley Recreational Grounds and Palmer Park, plus three field guns from the Great War.

Following this success, in response to Lord Beaverbrook's appeal, the WVS collected aluminium to make warplanes.

Scrap metal collected by the boys of Coley Council School. When the photo was taken they had salvaged five tons of paper and metal, raised £4 5s for the Spitfire Fund and collected £35 12s 2d for War Savings.

Within a few hours of the appeal, articles arriving at the WVS office included a collection of aluminium shoe trees, a vacuum cleaner, a shooting stick, a hair drier and duplicator. The total amount collected was 62 cwt.

Manpower was short and night driving was difficult. The council had a solution for both: paint white lines in the middle of the road using a machine. Another shortage was oil drums which the public were urged to return.

The government was aware of the air raid shelter shortage and promised to remedy the situation, but materials were in short supply. The problem was difficult to solve. In March, Reading Council announced the completion of public air raid shelters in Broad Street (2 shelters), Oxford Road, and Queen Victoria

Scouts played an important part in the country's salvage drive; these are scouts of the Anderson Troop from Anderson Baptist Church in Amherst Road. During the first year of the war, Reading Scouts collected more than 100 tons of waste paper and many tons of scrap iron.

Street, with trench shelters in Palmer Park and in Coley. This brought the total shelter provision to just over 9,000 places with 1,000 more in construction; school shelters could accommodate about 8,500 children and staff.

Many residents brought their dogs into town when they did their shopping. As the shelters were for people only, they would have to be abandoned in the road and left, frightened and distressed state, to their own devices. It was suggested that it was best to leave them at home.

If there was a raid, it was expected that many of the bombs would be incendiaries to start fires. Sand could be used to smother the oxygen from fires, but there was a shortage of sand, which the council was urged to address. The Mayor ordered

A family leaving their shelter after a daytime alert.

residents to clear their attics for ease of access if there was a bomb. Shortly after this every Reading household was given two sandbags on application to the ARP office and instructions on how to use them: three-quarters fill with dry sand or fine, dry, sifted soil, and when approaching the incendiary carry the sandbag as a shield, 'covering the face as a protection against flying sparks or fragments, and then throw the bag right on to the bomb'.

After a long wait the Ministry of Home Security announced that 1,300 small and 650 standard shelters would arrive soon. As the town needed shelters for 60,000 people, many homes would have to wait.

When shelters did arrive in April, they came with no nuts and bolts. The Mayor urged residents to set an example and put them up anyway. Where the nuts and bolts were to come from was not explained. There was a further problem: some householders were positioning them incorrectly and not following the instructions, making a lot of extra work for the Borough Surveyor's Department who irately told them to stop coming to him and talk to their local ARP warden.

Woodley had a shelter problem. It was no longer a village but a populous sprawling suburb with no public air raid shelter. Mothers were concerned for their children's safety, especially as their school was close to the aerodrome – they pointed out that the employees there had adequate protection. This had been an ongoing issue since October 1939 because the government did not define either Earley or Woodley as a vulnerable area. Financially this meant they had to buy their own shelter. However, in August Wokingham Council indicated that it would be prepared provide assistance to those earning less than £250 per annum.

For those who had the money and the time, an air raid shelter could be made quite comfortable, like this one.

No doubt many Reading households pondered on how to protect their pets during a gas attack. Fortunately the PDSA had an answer: gas proof safety kennels for small animals. There were two types: in one, the owner operated the bellows; in the second, automatic bellows were operated by the animal (how was not explained).

The matter of shelters was settled in June. No further Anderson shelters would be delivered to Reading once the original request had been filled: 13,500 when a known minimum of 14,700 were needed. Strangely, nearly 8,000 householders had not requested one and nearly 2,000 had been refused when they arrived.

It took nearly a year to work out how to find out about casualties after an air raid. Eventually a list was provided giving the addresses where the information could be obtained. Another issue, during and after a raid, was transport. The council agreed that buses would run until bombs actually fell on the town and if there was a raid warning before 10 pm the buses would run until midnight. Another problem was getting the people home from the town's shelters after a raid.

Then there was the problem of seating in the shelters. There was none and in September the Mayor publicly appealed for help. 'I invite Reading people to give boxes, wood, planks and chairs, or anything else they may think suitable.' He also wanted people to volunteer to join the 'Guild of Good Neighbours'. If there was a raid, members would offer hospitality in their homes for twenty-four hours to families who had been bombed out.

Home shelters could be as utilitarian or luxurious as the owners could afford. For those with the money, John Perring advertised emergency beds and bedding. They suggested a well filled pallet overlay for placing on a wooden base, a divan with spring centre overlay and solidly constructed base, or a range of mattresses to make the shelter a home from home.

Some evacuees went to America. In early October the Lund-Yates of Blenheim Road, Caversham, received good news. Their three children had arrived safely in New York though they had been bombed on the quayside waiting to board. It had cost them

£75 to secure their safety. A previous ship, the SS *Volendam,* carrying Reading children, had been torpedoed but fortunately there were no casualties and the children continued their journey on a different vessel or came home. The worst was the loss of the SS *Benares* and the deaths of 77 children, but none were from Reading. Churchill cancelled the trans-Atlantic evacuation programme shortly after this sinking.

Aboard the *Benares* was local teacher, Miss Mary Cornish, of Luckley School. She was one of forty survivors in her lifeboat who were at sea for eight days after the sinking. Her fellow passengers, men and six children, reported that she kept everyone's spirits up and that it was due to her that no one died. She was awarded the BEM for her work.

This is Miss Mary Cornish, of Luckley School, who was responsible for the survival of the forty survivors in her lifeboat after the SS Benares *was sunk. She received the BEM for her work. Of the 406 people aboard, 148 survived of which 19 were children; there had been 90 evacuees and 10 children travelling with parents.*

The continual arrival of new residents and the war industries contributed to a further shortage: water. Consumers were asked to restrict usage to keep reservoirs as full as possible, reducing the need to pump water, which used fuel. And full reservoirs meant fire-fighters had the water needed if there was a raid.

A full larder was essential after a raid. The Co-op recommended maintaining a store of canned foods. Naturally they had a wide range available and they would help with rationing: the ARP Complete Meal in a tin at 1s 1d was recommended. The next week they advised the town's residents to be prepared: 'KEEP WARM! During War conditions and Air Raids, Blankets may be scarce but C.W.S. Balloon Down Quilts are in good supply.'

Although everyone complained about the blackout and pedestrians were blamed for causing accidents, it created a popular form of entertainment: the blackout party, a popular, informal gathering round the fireside. In one, the food was an eat-as-you-please buffet, Danish style Smorrebrods were recommended, and for dessert a fresh fruit salad with cream and equal quantities of unsweetened evaporated milk were served.

The New Year list of honours included the name of a Reading man. Leading Seaman Purdue of 154 Caversham Road had been awarded the Distinguished Service Medal. He had been in the navy since 1932.

There was also the news that Charles Lovegrove, the well-known local undertaker, was married for the third time at the age of 84 to 70-year-old Eliza Kelly.

Although many saw the Sabbath as a day of rest, most were for having the choice of going to the cinema on a Sunday.

In February 1940, the council applied to Parliament for powers to enable them to allow cinematographic entertainment (movies) on Sundays. They were successful and a grateful public flocked to watch them, as these queues at two different cinemas show.

In February the council applied to Parliament to permit them to allow cinematograph entertainment on Sundays. This enabled troops in the town to use their spare time in a more controlled way; stalwarts wanted the shows to be for uniformed personnel and a guest. The application was successful and shortly afterwards local cinemas opened their doors to everyone on Sundays. *The Standard* carried a column advising readers what they could see.

During the Spanish Civil War, men from Reading voluntarily fought in the International Brigade. Some in Reading felt the same about the Finnish-Russian war. Ten old boys from Leighton Park School went to Finland with the Friends' Ambulance Unit in January. Later in the year Reading received three ambulances and three surgical unit cars from America paid for by well-wishers in America and Americans living in Britain.

As well as men, clothing was being asked for by Mignon Castle of Reckitt House, Leighton Park. When the Russians had attacked, many Finns fled with only the clothes they were wearing. Once again the good people of Reading were being asked to help the needy: children's clothing for Finland and men's, women's and children's clothing for Polish refugees in

This is the American ambulance convoy just after its arrival in the town. It was a gift to help in civil defence.

There was no end of ways to part people from their money: children were always a good choice. Here Tommy Eady, Iris Archer and Patricia Sibley of Waldeck Street are giving an open air concert in aid of wounded soldiers.

Romania and Hungary. The RSPCA asked for money to help Finnish army animals.

In the previous war, regional preferences had been shown to regiments or ships, providing them with clothing. Berkshire adopted a destroyer and all over the town and county, women, working in parties, knitted socks, scarves, helmets and other comforts for the crew. In Canada, an ex-Reading woman held the record for the most socks knitted: 110 pairs.

A more unusual request came from a Guardsman in France. He wanted readers of *The Standard* to send him make-up, men's and women's costumes and music. These were needed for the BEF concert party to improve their shows. In a similar vein, Lieutenant Appleton of Kenilworth Avenue asked for sports gear of any description to be sent to him for the 150 bored men he was stationed with somewhere in a remote district of England. And thirty-two soldiers from the Reading district stationed somewhere on the coast asked the readers of

National Savings had started early in the war; to keep track of how much was being saved a Victory ladder was positioned in Broad Street.

The Standard if they had a spare battery radio set they could have.

The government also hoped to get things for free. Relying on patriotism to achieve their aim, they asked for 125,000 pairs of binoculars for the armed forces, Mercantile Marine, Observer Corps, roof spotters and the Home Guard. They were prepared to pay a fair price but 'gifts would be warmly welcomed'. Although reported as good, Berkshire, Buckinghamshire, Hampshire, Kent, Oxfordshire, Surrey and Sussex only managed to provide 3,000 of the 33,000 gathered from across the country by February 1941.

The Red Cross requested help. It wanted people to donate spare used packs of playing cards for their convalescent homes.

Most of those receiving their call-up papers joined the colours but a small number refused. Reading became the regional centre for dealing with con-scientious objectors from Berkshire, Buckinghamshire, Hampshire, Oxford-shire, Sussex and part of Surrey. In the first hearing at the beginning of April, 53 men stated their case, 3 were totally exempted from military service, 7 received conditional exemption, 30 were registered for non-combatant duty, 13 were refused and one withdrew his application because he had joined the RAF. At the end of April there were 80 applicants for exemption, 60 of whom were from Oxford University.

However, the number of COs compared to the number enlisting was small. During the registration of the 1,690 25-year-old men from Newbury and Reading just 19 registered an

A novel way to raise money for the Red Cross is demonstrated here. T.L. Morley (goose-stepping) and H.G. Crook of the Park Institute Bowling Club are playing bowls in gas masks and steel helmets.

Initially the Home Guard wore their own clothes and an armband bearing the letters LDV (Local Defence Volunteers). They were then provided with a denim uniform and an arm band. As equipment became available the Home Guard began to look more like soldiers, which many of them had been. The armband was replaced by a shoulder title and primitive weapons were replaced by more modern guns. These local Home Guards are posing with their American rifles.

objection to military service. The figure fell for the 1911 class. When it was called up in June, of the 1,667 men called for only 11 were conscientious objectors.

The issue of conscientious objectors in council service was debated at the same time. By 26 votes to 20, the town council decided 'that those of their employees who were registered by the tribunals as conscientious objectors should be given leave of absence without pay for the duration of the war'. There was no doubt that many locals supported the council. The Wokingham Peace Pledge Union said that they had difficulty in renting rooms for their meetings. The council's attitude was entrenched. A few months later they refused to give a grant to a conscientious objector who wanted to train to be a teacher.

The council's decision was not met with universal acceptance. The Reading Society of Friends protested, reminding the council that conscientious objection was covered by an Act of Parliament and that such men had been passed by a tribunal. They deplored the curtailment of civil liberties shown by the action and were concerned that the decision might influence the outcomes of future tribunals. The decision was felt further afield. Margaret Bondfield from Southborough in Kent wrote to the paper commenting that the decision was a victory for intolerance and that it would weaken Home Front morale. A meeting of the Reading Railway Clerks' Association condemned the council's action as being undemocratic and seeking to interfere with the liberty of conscience allowed by the law.

The topic would not go away. The Minister of Labour told the council that he could not interfere with the tribunals but he felt that the council should alter their decision. At the next council meeting, after a lengthy debate, by 24 votes to 19 the council declined to rescind their decision.

Reading became the regional centre for many civil service departments. Like everyone else, civil servants were affected by rising prices and felt that, following the Great War's idea of wartime bonuses, they should receive one. They estimated everything cost 15 per cent more and were determined to receive a bonus, as had others who did not work for the government, pledging themselves to support a war bonus claim.

The increasing number of temporary residents to the town, especially servicemen, needed somewhere to stay. Toc H rented 160 Friar Street as a place where 'men of the services, and others transferred to Reading as a result of the war,' could 'find a welcome and the hand of friendship'. Named Talbot House, after the famous all-ranks club in Belgium during the Great War, it was open all day and every evening, staffed by volunteer helpers. Furniture was provided by the public, and upkeep and other costs were covered by donations.

Unlike in the Great War, Reading did not receive convoys of wounded men. But it was to be a hospital town for air raid casualties; the Royal Berks alone had over 400 beds available. With the start of the London Blitz, an ever increasing number of people left the city looking for safety in the Home Counties. Such was the influx that before the year was out Reading was declared closed to further incomers. However, in October Redlands Junior Department was closed, 'to prepare for the reception of a convoy of evacuated children from London'.

If 7-year-old Peter Garlick had had his way there would have been one more space available in Reading. He was an evacuee from Battersea living in Cholmley Road. Although he was quite happy in Reading and his 'auntie' and 'granny' were kind to him, he wanted to go home, and, as he liked walking, he set off. He was found at midnight walking along the Reading to London Road at Twyford. This was his fifth failed escape attempt. He was carried on a stranger's back all the way to Cholmley Road.

Reading was closed but, much to the chagrin of the citizens of Henley, their town was not. In March it was reported that in protest against proposals to send more evacuees to the town there was hooliganism and damage. With a population of 7,000 plus 750 official evacuees and 250 others, they protested to the Ministry to stop the arrival of a further 750.

Shortly after these complaints, thousands of local homes received a letter asking them to 'Join the Roll' of those who were willing to take children into their homes as the need arose.

The finger was pointed at Earley for not being prepared to take its fair share. In its defence it was pointed out that three-quarters of the houses were small and many were already overcrowded by evacuees; that the village's sanitary arrangements were primitive to the point of indecency; and that the cesspit provision was utterly inadequate to deal with the extra call upon its use by the population influx, with the result that many gardens have been flooded with sewage.

It was not only Earley. The Deputy Mayor of Reading expressed her disappointment at the town's response to the appeal to take in more evacuees. However, this did not stop nearly 2,000 more evacuees arriving.

One lady who would not be taking any evacuees was Mrs Esme Forrester, of 21 Derby Street. She was summoned at Reading Borough Police Court for neglecting her nine children aged between 10 months and 14 years. Between the ten occupants there was just one bed and a cot; the children were infested with vermin and had poor skin and hair but were fairly well nourished. As a result of illness and a husband in the army she had been unable to provide proper care. Taking her circumstances into account, she was bound over for a year with a probation officer to provide friendly supervision.

With Reading essentially closed to newcomers, the only way to replace men called up was to employ women and men who had been invalided out of the services. Phillips & Powis on Woodley aerodrome were proactive in this respect. In 1939 they began employing women as draughtsmen, and as the war continued increased their employment of women, 'unsurprisingly finding that they could do many jobs equally well, if not better, than men'. Huntley & Palmers needed labour and advertised for girls. As they would be coming from other districts they would need lodging, a problem in a closed town. The closing of their French factory in Paris, and escape of the English workforce and some French employees from Bayonne, provided them with some unexpected skilled labour.

The call-up of the young continued throughout the year for different age groups. First were men aged 20 to 24, followed by

26-year-olds. Eventually the register was extended to women. Although agricultural workers had to register they would not be called up. The age restriction did not stop underage boys getting into the war. Major Collett, the only son of a Reading police officer, was serving in the merchant navy at the age of 14.

There were many strangers in the town. To help make them feel more at home, the YMCA 'introduced a hospitality panel whereby soldiers… may have an opportunity of invitations singly or in pairs to some of the homes in Reading.' A number of people volunteered. Jewish soldiers in the area were already catered for. Since the beginning of the war, the Sir Herman Gollancz Hall in Goldsmid Road had been open to them.

Flight Lieutenant Arthur Hughes, eldest son of the Rev A. Price, a minister of Elm Park Hall, was in the papers after the award of the DFC for gallantry and devotion to duty. He survived the war.

The changing fortunes of the war affected the numbers in the town. Following the initial rush to leave London, the lack of German bombing encouraged many to return home. As a result, by June 'there were less than three-quarters of the total of evacuated children in Reading than at the commencement of the year.' The serious air attacks in the same month reversed the process. 'During the week 13th to 19th June alone nearly two thousand unaccompanied children were received into the town.' This continued throughout the year, quickly filling the town.

One incredible story was the release of a Reading woman from Germany. She was the governess of the two daughters of Princess Czartoryski in Poland when the war started. Miss Ida Daniels, of City Road, spent four months in Nazi jails before she was exchanged, along with eight other women and two 'coloured children', for German women prisoners. Two of her companions were Jewish governesses and the mother of the children was a trained manicurist. Their time in various prisons had not been pleasant, living on poor soup made from cabbages and potatoes, and black bread and water with margarine as a Sunday treat. They had to sleep in their clothes and only had one bath during their imprisonment. However, she reported that the Gestapo had treated them with respect.

This was followed in July by a similar story. Frederick Bailey, a film director, and ex-resident of Reading, was in Italy when Mussolini declared war on Britain. He had been given every co-operation to leave the country and was able to get to France through Switzerland. Although the train he was on was bombed and machine-gunned he eventually arrived in Bordeaux. From there he went to a fishing port, Le Verdun, where the fishing boat he was to escape on was sunk. Bombed and machine-gunned again while waiting on the dunes, he was fortunate. A British cruiser was close by when a Dutch cargo vessel was refusing to take British people on board. An Imperial Airways wireless operator who was with him took a motor boat and went to the cruiser for help. A boarding party took control of the Dutch vessel and took it back to Britain.

 Working hours in the Miles aircraft factory were long because of the continual need for planes. In May a government directive demanded that aircraft factories work seven days a week, twenty-four hours a day. Workers had every eighth day off and changed between day and night shifts on alternate months. Such pressure could not be maintained indefinitely and a year later it reverted to the standard 47 hour week starting at 07.55hrs and finishing at 17.30hrs. The night shift clocked on at 20.30hrs and finished the next morning at 07.30hrs. Weekend working was restricted to Saturday mornings but when the need arose many worked on Sundays. Continuous working was brought back before the invasion of Europe. Rates of pay were high compared to many other local industries.

To make sure that everything would function efficiently during a raid, an extensive civil defence exercise was held in March across the south of England from Slough to the coast. It was planned at the regional office in Reading and involved

The ARP held regular practices throughout the war. Here they are rescuing an injured civilian from under wreckage.

ARP workers, auxiliary firemen and policemen from Berkshire, Buckinghamshire, parts of Dorset, Hampshire, Oxfordshire and Surrey. Slough was one of the designated bombed towns and Reading sent teams of ARP workers to help deal with casualties. Reading also sent twenty-four firemen with pumps.

Air raid warnings were often given during the day. As a result schools had air raid practices on a regular basis, in some schools every other day. School children also had to carry their own gas mask once they reached the age of 5.

If the shelter was not in the school grounds, as at Christ Church School where it was in the Tank (Spring Gardens Play Area on Spring Terrace at the top of the west side of Whitley Street), then children would run home instead and risk being punished on their return to school. However, in general children living less than five minutes away from home were allowed to

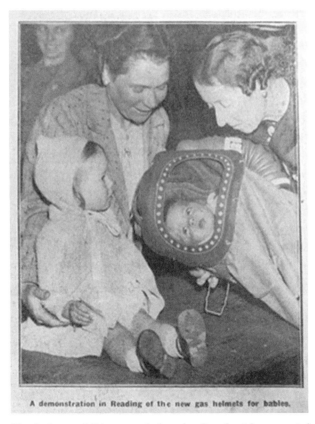

A demonstration in Reading of the new gas helmets for babies.

Newly-born children needed to be fitted with a special gasmask which was difficult to fit and carry around.

go home. The logbook of Redlands Junior Department for September reads: 'Air raid warnings were sounded during morning sessions, yesterday and today. Children were dispersed into houses near the school and returned as soon as all clear sounded.' By the end of the year, with shelters installed in the grounds, the children could shelter very quickly with just a few, at the wish of their parents, going home.

Wilson School, after four days practice, got the time down to four minutes for all the children to be in the closest shelter, and four months later it was down to three minutes. The problem was that the shelter only held about fifty children; the remainder had to disperse to various houses for shelter. The council's excuse was that the building materials were needed for 'more important' works. An anxious parent thought that was an insult to the children.

With a daylight alarm there was the problem of what to do with the children in the shelter. Often it was a lesson, with pre-planned activities to make it a continuation of the school day. As well as parlour games, time in the dark and poorly-ventilated shelters was used to reinforce the times tables. Some children knitted comforts for the troops in the shelter. They also practised wearing their gas masks.

Gas masks were inspected periodically by the ARP to check they were still in good condition. To help keep the mask in good condition, especially those of children, it was suggested that a cover be purchased for little cost, or knitted. Instructions were provided in the paper with the suggestion of putting two straps on the cover so it could be worn like a satchel. For those with money to spare, the smartest mask cases were made out of black patent leather, retailing at ten shillings.

Allegedly the staff of this unnamed Reading store always had their gas masks handy, and when the camera man called, visitors and staff donned their respirators for the picture.

In a 'full' town where every manufacturing business was working overtime, there were still unemployed in the town. In March 1,690 people were without work and in April 1,456. One employer constantly advertising for people was the NAAFI. As the forces grew in size so too did it. There were also many other situations vacant.

Transport to work was not guaranteed. It was unreliable because people flagged down buses between stops and behaved in an unruly way. A queuing system for buses had been suggested and by-laws had been passed which dictated how people should queue, how they boarded a bus and what might happen if they did not observe the regulations. How effective this was is shown by a comment in August from Maurice Titcomb of Windermere Road. He questioned whether the by-law had been adopted and if so why it was not enforced, concluding that, in his experience, those at the front of the queue were not assured a place and that the only guarantee of a seat was 'a pair of energetically used elbows'. The situation had not changed by Christmas when a Londoner who came to the town regularly complained that locals displayed a 'deplorable lack of decency' in bus queues, referring to hooligans and savages, and wondering if they would ever form orderly queues like Londoners.

A night time alert could affect the next day's productivity, and in the case of children reduce their attendance. On one morning in September, attendance at Christ Church School was as low as forty-eight per cent. In consequence of the raids, 'the Education Committee decided that Reading's schools should not close their registers until 10.30 am.' When a raid took place after midnight, it could delay the start of the school day.

With the expectation of a raid locals received advice from the ARP based on the experiences of a Spaniard who had experienced raids in the Spanish Civil War:

1. At the sound of the alarm, keep a cool head, follow instructions, and do not rush.
2. Always know the shortest road to the nearest air raid shelter. Have warm clothing with you in winter.

3. If there is no shelter available, get down into a basement. Keep close to corners. AVOID BEING NEAR DOORS AND WINDOWS.
4. If no warning has been given against gas, keep your doors and windows open. Do not stand in the middle of the room, but get close to the main outside walls.
5. If actual bombing finds you in the street, rush into the nearest doorway, lie down flat close to the wall, with head pointing inwards.
6. If caught in the open, far from any shelter or house, lie flat on the lowest ground; if there is grass or soft ground, lie there. Bombs falling in soft ground sink in and the explosion is upwards.
7. Carry with you a lead pencil, piece of soft rubber, or a cork to put between your teeth, in order to keep the mouth open. This avoids internal injury, or the bursting of the ear drums by concussion.
8. If lying in the open, cover your head with a folded coat or an open book to avoid injuries from splinters from anti-aircraft shells.
9. For information. A bomb falling in the immediate vicinity makes a loud WHISTLING sound. Bombs falling 100 to 500 yards distant make a loud HISSING sound.

The ARP Controller stated that No. 7 saved thousands from having burst ear drums.

The threat of an air raid anytime anywhere did not stop people taking holidays. Although adverts asked people not to travel unless it was necessary, the Great Western put on extra trains to the coast. Travellers had to apply for emergency ration books in order to eat on their vacation.

Among the new arrivals in the town were some destined for jail. 'In August 1940, a party of lads who had survived the bombing of Portland Borstal were transferred to Reading.' In mid-October most were moved to another detention centre with those due for release left behind to clean the prison. Shortly after it had been vacated, it was handed over to the Canadian army as a detention prison with warders who carried sub-machine guns. As it had not been used as a prison since 1919, conditions inside were primitive, with no electric light or sanitation. Future occupants were mostly petty criminals, but after VE-Day it held some notorious prisoners.

Was there some correlation between Reading Jail becoming a Canadian prison and the regular reports about the poor behaviour of Canadian troops in the area? A typical story was that of five Canadian soldiers visiting Bradbury Bros. While buying various soldiers' necessities they managed to remove a leather belt and four pairs of gloves. They had been drinking and after being told they should be ashamed of their conduct were fined 10s with 1s costs.

The call-up of younger men affected Home Defence. To replace them men aged 35 to 50, whether they had previous military experience or not, were urged to join the Royal Berkshire Regiment Home Defence Battalion. Their job was to guard railways, roads and other vulnerable points. They were soon to be replaced by the Home Guard.

With the possibility of a German invasion, the government formed the Local Defence Volunteers (LDV) – later to become the Home Guard. Many of the volunteers were ex-soldiers, with some previously high ranking officers becoming mere platoon commanders. They were not all old or had previous military experience. In February 1941, *The Standard* published a photo of the youngest member, 12-year-old Michael Tate of Oxford Road. He was a messenger and was on duty five times a week, wearing an arm band to show he was a member of the Home Guard.

Although the minimum age for joining the Home Guard was 17, somehow Michael Tate, aged 12, became a messenger for his local company.

Reading felt the invasion threat when a defensive line was built south of the town. Across Berkshire pillboxes and checkpoints suddenly appeared. *The Standard* helpfully included drawings of the planes German parachutists would descend from. An ex-Reading resident, the vice-president of a gold mine in Canada, and an ex-soldier, wrote to say that the area was worth dying for. But he was over 4,000 miles away and too old to fight.

The seriousness of the situation was described by ex-Brigadier General E.J. Phipps-Hornby, commanding Sonning Platoon of the LDV. Although he was addressing Sonning, it was the same in Reading. 'The Village of Sonning, like a large number of other villages in England, Scotland and Wales has been put in a state of defence. Pill boxes and sandbags fortments (sic) have been placed at certain points. Some people take it as a joke that Sonning should ever be attacked, but this is far from the case. I am far from being a pessimist. I am confident, in the end, we shall win, but only if everyone of us take a hand in defeating the Germans. To do that it is the duty of every man who calls himself a man, to take his place in the defence of his village and his home. I appeal to every man in Sonning between the ages of 17 and 65 to join the L.D.V.s at once. We want every man we can get.'

The men of Reading too young or old to serve, and those whose employment stopped them serving, were keen to join the new force. It was formed on 14 May, and three days later 700 parashooters (or parashots as they were called initially) had enrolled in Reading alone. A week later the number was double. Woodley aerodrome had its own unit and was further protected by anti-aircraft defences and the camouflaging of the entire factory and aerodrome. Huntley & Palmers recruited its own 'armed posse'.

LDV members were identified by armbands because of the shortage of uniforms. When uniforms were available, they were not always suitable for night work. For the better off this was not a problem, but not everyone was able to supplement their uniform with warming garments. Like those in need at sea, people were asked to knit for the LDV; this time wool was to be provided: knitted pullovers, scarves – like Pike's in *Dad's Army* – and mittens were needed.

There was no compulsion, but every able-bodied man was strongly encouraged to join. Again the words of General Phipps-Hornby: 'There are still a few men in and around Sonning Village who have not as yet joined the L.D.V. Perhaps they think it unnecessary to do so. They may think there is no chance of an attack on this village. That may be so. On the other hand a sure way to prevent any attack, that may be made, from being successful is to be prepared for it. No man can help in the defence unless he has been trained, knows his place, how to get to it and what to do when he gets there. No man would be allowed at the last moment to join in the defences who had not received previous training. He would be a greater danger to his own side than to the enemy. In speaking of the defence of Sonning we are not so much thinking of bricks and mortar as of the honour of our women and children. Surely no man, when he realises what is at stake, will hold back for one minute. We ask every man to join us NOW.'

The Berkshire Home Guard was a land force but, as the Thames ran through the county, a waterborne unit, the Upper Thames Patrol, was raised to guard against saboteurs and the enemy. With headquarters at Moss's Boathouse, the unit patrolled the Thames from Teddington to Lechlade. In September it advertised for volunteers with river experience and for the loan of launches and cabin cruisers. Although a Home Guard unit trained as infantry, the 'Inland Marines' wore a more practical naval style of dress. It was not provided by the government so had to be purchased privately. To raise funds, an all-star matinee was given at the Palace Theatre in Reading. The performers included Alice Delysia, Tommy Handley, Trefor Jones, Margaret Eaves, Thomas Best, Will Kings and Mr Flotsam and Mr Jetsam, together with the band of the Royal Berkshire Regiment.

Readers' familiarity with *Dad's Army* belies the dangers of being in the Home Guard. Many were killed during the war. John Butcher, a 17-year-old schoolboy, was unlucky while on patrol. Someone accidentally discharged their weapon in his direction, wounding him in the abdomen; he died four days later in the Royal Berks.

Meanwhile in the same hospital, a 7-year-old girl, Ann Shilton, died after being knocked down by a car in Robin Hood Lane in Winnersh; and on 19 March, Jill Slade, one of twins, was born prematurely, weighing just 2 lb 10 oz. She was the youngest of ten children and was regarded as the miracle of Dulvertson Gardens. In the hospital she was regularly massaged with olive oil, wrapped in cotton wool and placed in a cardboard box, constantly heated by hot water bottles. By August she was declared to be a perfectly normal baby.

In July Private MacDonald of the LDV fired two shots at a car which did not stop when challenged. The car had misfired and he had taken that for the signal to shoot. Fortunately no one was hurt. In the same week Private Niblett waved a cyclist down. When he did not slow down he pulled him off his bike.

Other organisations wanted slightly older men for a different form of home defence. St. Giles's School in London Road was a combined recruiting office and in May men between 30 and 45 of good physique and intelligence were urgently required as balloon operators. With mounting casualties, the RAF began advertising for those about to be conscripted to volunteer instead for flying duties, but only if they were fit, intelligent, and possessed dash and initiative.

To delay German troops if they were to invade, towns and cities were told to obliterate anything that could give the enemy a clue as to their whereabouts. Road signs were removed and some were painted or covered over. The word Berkshire in the Royal Berks Hospital was blacked over, and 'The proprietor of Shinfield Fisheries found himself in court for failing to [remove the word Shinfield], even though his business was some two miles from the settlement of that name.'

Although in short supply, because of sea mines, U-boats sinking fishing boats, and trawlers being used by the Royal Navy, fish was never put on ration and attempts to substitute whale meat for fish was not popular. Margaret Fairburn, the youngest in her family, recalled her regular Saturday morning job. It was to 'queue outside a fish shop in Wokingham Road with a carrier bag and newspaper to buy any fish and as much as I was offered'.

As well as needing men for the LDV, there was also a need for defensive positions for them to man in case of an invasion. At the request of the Ministry of Labour, Suttons sent a team of twelve men to work on military defences being constructed near Pangbourne in July. The next month they were asked if they could assist the local Fuel Overseer. This aid was to prove profitable: 6d a ton for storage and the cost of the restoration of the land was met by the government. After discussions, a piece of ground at the company's sports ground on Cintra Avenue was selected for the storage of 1,000 tons of coal; a profit of £25 for doing very little.

Huntley & Palmer also provided paid labour to help build defence works. Their first job was to fill sandbags, 19,800 of them, which their lorries transported to defensive positions around the town. At the same time a register of volunteers prepared to assist with defence works was being compiled.

The LDV were not the only soldiers in Reading. Ranikhet Camp in Tilehurst, named after a hill station in India used by the Royal Berkshire Regiment, was constructed to accommodate over 1,000 men. It was built quickly on land stretching from Church End Lane and taking in the area now bounded by Combe Road, Poole Close, Elvaston Way and Stanham Road. Newly conscripted men had been billeted in the town but as each hut became available they were moved to the new camp for ten weeks' basic training before leaving for Blandford Camp. On completion it became a Primary Training centre. In 1943, the 327th Glider Infantry, part of the American 101st Airborne Division were stationed there, and later it was used to house families with no accommodation, and in a separate section, PoWs.

There were other American troops in the town later in the war. G. Selway remembers as a child sitting on a wall opposite the Three Tuns pub watching black Americans from Bulmershe Court go in, followed by American soldiers from Whiteknights and Canadians from Brock Barracks. There were fights at the weekends with the white Americans attacking the blacks; the white Canadians sided with the black soldiers. The Military Police along Wilderness Road 'allowed the fighting to go so far before driving in and breaking it all up'.

As the war escalated more local men became PoWs. The Red Cross was given the task of providing them with regular parcels. There were also regular meetings of the families of those affected and regular collections of money to help provide materials.

Money was collected by the government through National Savings Certificates, defence bonds and savings deposits, and throughout the war people were told to be aware of the 'Squanderbug' who was working for the Nazis to encourage people to spend money on unnecessary purchases rather than save it to help the war effort. A National Savings Week in May featured dancing in the Forbury with prizes and speeches and a travelling cinema. In the twenty-one weeks since the scheme started, to 25 May, Reading had saved £717,296 to help the war effort, an average of £34,157 a week. During the Savings Week, Reading saved a record £45,558. As in the Great War, a marker was set up in the centre of the town to show how well the town was saving. A month later, the total had risen to £1,024,658.

The next attack on Reading's pockets was the purchase of a Spitfire; the cost was £5,000. In two weeks the Mayor had raised just a quarter of the cost; slow in comparison with later fundraising events. By the end of September they had bought the engine and two guns. A week later, and a further £350 saved, an air screw could be purchased. To increase donations, a captured German plane was to be brought to Reading and displayed in the Odeon's car park; people were to be allowed to inspect the interior of the plane for a donation to the fund. It had the desired effect, raising £504. By 18 October £3,640 15s 5d had been raised, with the fund closing at the end of October. The fund was still £994 short on 25 October, £550 remained to be collected on 31 October, and on 8 November the shortfall was £170. On 15 November, Reading reached its total and more, but this did not stop the campaign. By Christmas the fund had reached £5,255 16s 5d.

Before they had even bought the wings for the Spitfire, the Mayor was appealing for money for War Weapons Week, starting

9 November. He wanted to raise £400,000 in bonds (quickly upped to £450,000) and savings certificates to cover the cost of a destroyer that would become HMS *Reading*; around £4 a head. The ship, which served in the Atlantic, was not bought with the money. It was admitted in the papers that it had been exchanged for bases that the Americans could use and was over twenty years old. The tagline for the week was 'Shell out and smash the "Hit" out of Hitlerism.' In Reading's biggest effort so far a range of activities was arranged: parades, a special matinee at the Palace Theatre with admission by War Savings Stamps purchased in the theatre, a ceremony in St. Mary's Butts, a football match, a 'Hunt the Letters' competition for shoppers, and an exhibition of wartime photographs – 'The Air Arm of Britain'. Amazingly, the day before the week officially began, there were promises of £418,650. Like the Spitfire fund end date, one week became two and by 22 November the town had raised £851,319.

At the same time many Reading workers joined the Red Cross Penny-a-Week Fund to provide weekly parcels to PoWs. It was inexpensive individually but across the country it raised thousands of pounds every week. Some Reading pubs joined in, with darts players fining themselves every time they failed to score more than ten with three darts. Such was the success of the scheme that £5,635 15s was raised by the middle of 1942.

Not everyone in the town was behind the war effort. During the savings campaign two local men were detained under the defence regulations: Percy Bates, cycle and wireless dealer of 88 Northcourt Avenue, a well-known member of the British Union of Fascists, and A. Woodgate, another member. Percy's brother Herbert, also a fascist, had applied to the tribunal as a conscientious objector. The tribunal decided he had no conscientious objections and was sent for military service. Ernest Chandler of Queen's Road was fined £5 for making negative comments about the Royal Navy, the King and the government, such as '--- the King and country…The British Navy are a rotten lot of cut-throats…Churchill was a murderer, and Bevin and Morrison should be shot.' Chandler asked if he would have to go to prison if he couldn't pay the fine; he was told by the chairman

Before people spent all their money on Christmas presents, Reading held a War Weapons Week, with the aim of raising £450,000. The money would enable the purchase of a destroyer, to be named HMS Reading. Actually it was an American lend/lease ship built in 1919 and had cost nothing.

Even before event started, £449,000 had been promised towards HMS Reading.

of the bench, Colonel Barker, that he could go to prison straight away if he wanted.

Gypsies were singled out for their lack of patriotism by Wokingham Council. People had been collecting scrap and leaving it in piles along the Reading Road in Winnersh only to find that the best pieces had been stolen. But a scrap dump was game to anyone, not just gypsies. In Henley, Alfred Buckett was fined 15s for stealing a copper copper from the dump to mend his own copper.

At the same time Reading was giving a welcome to the evacuated men from Dunkirk. Hospitality was extended to hundreds of men, including French and Belgians, on their way to other destinations. Many passed through the Reading Services Club in London Street where they were fed and provided with a bath and bed. Two nearly stayed in Reading for some time but for the leniency of the judge: they stole a car in Broad Street and drove off without putting the lights on. They were apprehended but because of their ordeal in France they got off with a single payment of 7s 6d for costs.

During the summer months, one pleasant way of passing a day off was a boat trip. These continued to run throughout the war and offered a cheap day out with a return from Caversham lock to Wallingford costing 3s 6d or 2s 6d from Caversham Bridge hotel to

Henley. For the better off, Smith's coaches were still running trips to Brighton, Hindhead, Bournemouth and Whipsnade Zoo. There was always greyhound racing on Saturday, Monday and Wednesday evenings. For those who were light of foot there were dancing classes at the County School of Dancing and every Saturday there was dancing at the Olympia.

There was always a good book. Lists of the new books available at Reading library were published and the papers carried articles on what they felt were good reads. The library was doing its best to cope under wartime circumstances: changed hours due to lighting restrictions; a large increase in the number of children using the libraries – and adults too; storing safely the valuable, rare and irreplaceable items in the local collection. Staff numbers had been depleted but this impacted mainly the branch libraries; Central Library continued with the pre-war working hours. Even with the financial restrictions it still managed to add nearly 7,000 new books to its stock.

Patting themselves on the back, they were proud that the number of loans was 620,775 as against the record of 623,958 in the year 1938-39; children borrowed 173,440 books. Of the six libraries, the busiest was Central, followed by east and south. The least used library was Tilehurst. Across the borough, the number of borrowers rose by nearly 4,000 to 27,828.

Couples continued to get married. Clothing was not yet rationed, allowing the bride a chance to shine on her big day. Three examples give an idea of the clothes being worn. Mr Lovett from Tooting married Miss K. Emmons of King's Meadow. The bride wore a clover morocain dress with brown hat, gloves and shoes. Her attendant wore saxe blue, with morocain navy hat, gloves and shoes. Leaving for her honeymoon in Brighton she wore a green costume with fox fur. At her wedding to the assistant manager of Heelas, Molly Pearce wore a blue ensemble with brown hat, and carried a shower bouquet of soft mauve and pink sweet peas. Given away by her father, Doris Anderson of Briants Avenue wore an ankle-length dress of ivory satin with a head-dress of orange blossom with a short veil, and carried a bouquet of white carnations and white heather. Leaving for her honeymoon in Chalfont St. Peters she wore a dress of Alpine rose moss crêpe with hat to match and camel-hair coat.

Charity work became a normal part of life, and on 6 July Sir Felix and Lady Pole held a Midsummer Fair and Shakespearean Masque in the gardens of Calcot Place. The event was in aid of what is now known as The Children's Society, but was originally founded as The Waif and Strays Society.

Fire brigades across the country realised that in the case of a major raid inter-brigade cooperation would be essential; nearby brigades were put on the alert, ready to assist. This cooperation also applied to small stations like Sonning. On 7 September, the brigade was called to report to a fire station in West London at 21.30hrs where they joined other brigades. They proceeded through London to the dock area where they were bombed by the Germans during seven hours of continuous pumping. They arrived back at 16.30hrs the next day. The brigades went wherever there was a need. They went from London straight on to Birmingham.

Although not a major raid, a bomb landed near the Blagrave Branch Hospital on 5 November. It only damaged the boiler house but a 'time bomb some 30 feet away necessitated the temporary evacuation of 40 patients to the main hospital'. A month earlier the Germans had attempted to bomb Reading aerodrome; presumably they meant to hit Woodley. Then they tried to bomb Hatfield aerodrome where they were shot down.

Reading was again lucky on the night of 27/28 November. During a series of raids against London and Plymouth some enemy aircraft failed to find their targets, dropping their bombs near Reading. There was no damage or casualties, just craters.

Woodley suffered two casualties in five raids: in the first on 16 August an aircraft was destroyed, and one person was slightly injured on 6 October. Marjorie Culham witnessed the second raid: 'the sirens went off at teatime. I was at a party in a friend's house in Wokingham Road, we heard a plane and rushed into the back garden and watched it circle round and then head off in the Woodley direction. It dropped four bombs and then disappeared from sight (it was like a chicken laying eggs!).' Bombs also fell in the countryside around the town, probably

This is 81 Cardiff Road after the air raid on 26 November. There were no casualties.

not deliberately. Their victims were cows: one dead, and two injured which had to be destroyed. On the same day as Earley's first raid, 12 September, Woodley was again bombed, causing heath fires at South Lake. The airfield was attacked again on 16 September, and on 3 and 6 October.

Earley felt the brunt of the Luftwaffe on more than one occasion. On 12 September three bombs were dropped on the GWR line north of the gasworks. At the end of the month, six bombs were dropped on Sutton's Trial Grounds and three on Erleigh Court Gardens. On 12 October, four bombs exploded in and near Bulmershe Woods. A different source states that one bomb fell 'on Bulmershe Park, a second exploded in Milton Road, damaging several houses. Another scored a direct hit on a fish pond in Erleigh Court Gardens scattering fish everywhere! And a fourth hit Sutton's trial grounds.' In 1970, bomb disposal experts were called to defuse a bomb that had been found at the corner of Radstock and Redhatch Drive. An oil bomb was dropped on Earley on 1 December but appears to have caused no damage.

On 5 November, twenty-three bombs were dropped northwest of Blagrave Hospital in Tilehurst, but little damage was caused.

Sutton's main premises were in the town and considered vulnerable to incendiaries. A fire-watching group was formed with extra payment to ensure volunteers. Employee John Cox recalls that 'the assembly point was Abbey Hall, King's Road. An employee warehouseman/fireman living locally was appointed to be in charge of the company's manual fire engine, complete with hose reels, buckets of water, hydrants and other equipment.' Buckets were filled with sand, others with water and 'stirrup pumps and shovels which staff had been trained to use were placed at strategic points round the firm and where accessible on roofs. A small shed was erected on the roof overlooking the Market Place, which gave the fire-watchers some protection from the weather and a commanding view over the town. It was also a good vantage-point for the aircraft spotters.'

The fire-watchers patrolled the factory on arranged routes throughout the night using dimmed torches. When the siren went, all points were manned and a director sent for; he was to take charge. Living some distance away he would arrive by 'bicycle, tin-helmet over his shoulder, still in his pyjamas'.

Although Reading and surroundings had been bombed with no casualties, that did not mean that no Reading citizens were killed by air raids. Two were killed on 15 October with a third dying of injuries the next day in an air raid in London where they had been working. This was two weeks after the first raid on Reading.

On 1 October, nine high explosive bombs fell across Caversham causing minor damage and two days later Coley was the target for four small high explosive bombs causing minor damage to a number of properties. Bombs fell just outside the borough boundary on 9 October and 15 November, while on 26 November high explosive and incendiaries fell on Reading and Caversham. This latter raid was the worst of the Blitz period, causing the destruction of two houses in Cardiff Road with damage to three other homes.

There were more blackout-related motor vehicle accidents. 'With no street lighting and greatly reduced apertures for the headlights, motorists' found it extremely difficult to drive at night, but they continued to do so. Those injured were initially taken to the Royal Berks, but such was their number that from June 1940 crashes were divided geographically: those in the western parts of Reading were dealt with by Battle, those in the east by the Royal Berks.

Pedestrians also struggled with the blackout. While some trees, lampposts and kerbstones were painted white, and low-light torches could be used, once away from the town centre the roads became very dark and accidents were common. Ada Little (née Mears), while off duty from her Air Raid Warden activities, recalled walking into a brick wall during the blackout, sustaining two black eyes that lasted a week.

Accidents happened during the day too. While on her way to school, Jean Wilson, aged 11, of Stockton Road, was crossing the Basingstoke Road when she was knocked down by a milk van. Seriously injured, she was taken to the Royal Berks where she died later in the day.

Although the Royal Berks had initially benefitted from the extra money provided by the EMS, by spring 1940 there was a deficit of £11,000; the result of the rising number of patients, constantly increasing prices and higher wages. The hospital decided to use its buildings as a security for a bank overdraft and close over 100 beds at a time when they were full. Through the newly established Regional Hospitals Council, Berkshire County Council agreed to grant the hospital £5,000, with a grant of £1,000 from Reading Borough Council. With these grants, the money from EMS, and increased support from public benefactors, the hospital was solvent by the end of the year.

The families of those killed, wounded, missing or PoW were informed officially and the information published in the papers. Lists could be found in the pages of the *China Dragon*, the Royal Berkshire Regiment's journal, for those serving in the regiment. Notification of a missing loved one being a PoW was a relief: they were safe. But not always: taken prisoner at

Dunkirk, the Gardiners of Anathoth in Earley were informed in late November that their son had died on 1 August.

At the end of September, the King and Queen paid an informal visit to the Kennylands camp school at Kidmore End which housed 200 evacuees from the Beale Modern School in Ilford. After an hour's visit they left.

Autumn turned people's thoughts to staying warm, especially as they knew there would a shortage of coal. Langstons of West and Cork Street asked residents to get ready for the cold by purchasing plenty of warm clothing. Naturally they had the products everyone needed, and if purchasing in September, customers would beat the latest increase in taxation – purchase tax.

The Poppy Day collection in 1939 had raised £1,772 2s 11d, excluding considerable church collections. The target for

In September the King and Queen paid a visit to Kennylands Camp School at Kidmore End. For an hour they looked around the camp and inspected the pupils of Beale Modern School from Ilford.

1940 was double last year's, but by 15 November it had only reached £2,003 1s 7d. As in 1939 there was no service at the war memorial.

The second Christmas of the war was bleaker than the first. Even the vicar of Sonning felt unable to wish his readers a merry Christmas, merely sending them his best blessings for the great festival, again emphasising the peace and goodwill aspect of the celebration. Even the blackout conspired against it with lighting only allowing for one early morning service.

The blackout affected wines and spirits selling times. Firms such as Fergusons on Broad Street had to close at 6 pm. However, to allow people to buy their festive drinks, special licences were issued allowing the sale of alcohol continuously through the day from 10 am to 6 pm with no afternoon closing. Unlike in the Great War, so far there was no shortage of alcohol on sale. Higg's Brewery on Castle Street asked customers to stock up early. They were offering over twelve wines, twelve spirits, sixteen varieties of ales and stouts in three sizes, and a range of cask beers and ciders in 4½ or 9 gallon barrels. There would be some Christmas cheer around, particularly at Simonds Brewery: it had been given a Royal Warrant during the year and was paying a 14½ per cent dividend. But some of the town's pubs reported a shortage.

There were plenty of films to see over the month. The Rex on Oxford Road was showing six different films in just one week, while at the Regal in Caversham there were eight films to choose from.

While the citizens of Reading could be entertained and purchase alcohol easily, there was more difficulty with everyday necessities, as the Co-op noted in a late November advert cleverly entitled 'A study in Black and White'. The reason, coal deliveries could not exceed five cwt per fortnight and milk could not be delivered until after 7.30 am because milk supplies were still short. How late delivery helped was not explained.

The opening on 11 December of the People's Pantry was an important event attended by local dignitaries. The menu was supposed to provide an ample meal for sixpence. However, on the official opening a typical meal was ninepence. What they

IT'S DOING
HITLER'S
WORK

KILL THAT RAT!

In the Great War there had been sparrow and vermin hunts with rewards for catching or killing the pests. Hitler's face was easy to parody and he was used as the face of the rat which the public were informed were as damaging to food supplies as the U-boat.

received was substantial: soup, steak and kidney pie or braised lamb, with potatoes and beans, followed by apple pie or syrup roll with a cup of tea. The enterprise was staffed by the WVS. What was not known at the time was how important the building would become in the history of the town during the war.

As Christmas approached, Tuck's encouraged the sending of cards to family and friends across the Empire. They had a range of over 1,000 to choose from and a 'large supply of delightful calendars' for Christmas gifts.

The sending of parcels of essentials would be useful to PoWs but they had to be sent through the Red Cross and only contain certain goods. Sending them privately breached the blockade, was in breach of the Trading with the Enemy Acts and was likely to assist the enemy. Probably more important to the sender was that they were unlikely to reach their destination.

Much transported food would not reach its destination. According to the Ministry of Agriculture and Fisheries, during the previous war rats 'ate and destroyed more food than was sunk in the four years by German U-boats.' In the week before Christmas, National Rat Campaign was launched: total war against rats was declared with everyone expected to do their best to get rid of the pests using cats, dogs, ferrets, traps, poisons and gasses. The campaign was launched with a rat sporting a Hitler moustache.

With Christmas days away, adverts were focused on 'really useful Xmas gifts'. Lewis and Hyland in London Street had fur-lined foot-muffs and extra-large floor pouffes at pre-war prices. Time was limited for purchasing presents as shops closed for the usual half-day on Wednesday before Christmas as well as on Christmas and Boxing Day.

Few companies took out advertising space for Christmas greetings. Two exceptions were E. Jackson & Son of Jackson's Corner, who extended Season's Greetings to their customers at home and in the forces. Great Western Motors wished their customers and employees 'Good Wishes, Good Hope and Good Cheer' and added a positive message about the coming years. 'We face the future with quiet confidence, and in the belief that, however hard or long the road we have to travel may be, its end will be victory, and with it Peace, Happiness and Prosperity.' Vincent's garage on Station Square told readers it had nearly 100 cars in stock, including low mileage 1939 models.

The Mayor felt it 'a proud and happy privilege to offer greetings to the people of Reading at this Christmas time. No one is more conscious than I of the wide sense of duty and the many sacrifices made on all sides to serve the community. My greetings are, therefore, at the same time, an expression of profound thanks for this great and wonderful voluntary spirit. I feel that the community spirit is greater to-day than ever before in the history of our town, and in offering my good wishes I feel that I am doing so in a more intimate and friendly way and not in a formal and official manner. This sense of comradeship and unity of purpose is something which cannot be beaten.'

To assist parents who were unable to provide winter clothing for their children, and for evacuees, warm clothing was requested. Helpers waited for unwanted clothing to alter for use by those less privileged.

There was some good news from the Chief Constable of Berkshire. In his quarterly report he noted a drop in burglary, housebreaking and shop breaking. The bad news was that many of the crimes had been committed by juveniles and even worse by evacuees. There was further bad news, more people had been killed on the roads but fewer injured.

The government announced a Christmas bonus: during Christmas week housewives would receive 'for each ration coupon 12 ozs. of sugar and 4 ozs. of tea'. Normal rationing

Christmas meant selling, and all the major shops advertised and wished their customers, past and present, the season's greetings.

would continue the following week, and no fresh or tinned fruit would be imported for some time apart from a limited quantity of oranges.

Each issue of *The Standard* featured the week's latest casualties. The 27 December edition reported three deaths and eighteen taken prisoner. Information was requested on Private John Earp of Tidmarsh Street who had been missing since May. Private May, missing since May, was reported as safe in Switzerland.

Unlike the vicar of Sonning, the editor of the *China Dragon* finished the year on an upbeat note. 'We wish all ranks of the Regiment a Happy New Year. The coming year will, no doubt, be a momentous one in the history of our Empire. 1941 will decide Victory and Peace.' Whether many would have agreed with this hope is unlikely, but most would have agreed with what he wrote next: 'Let us therefore prepare ourselves for a tremendous effort…to fight hard we must live and train hard.'

Karandash, writing in *The Standard,* initially had a different take on the year. 'We have come to the end of a year which, in many respects, may be regarded as the most disastrous of our history.' However, later in the piece, after extolling the virtues of the armed forces, he noted that the country had stood up against the forces of evil to maintain freedom of thought and speech, of justice and of truth. He believed that the country was happier for their struggles.

Noting that the New Year would be rung in once again without bells, *The Standard* quoted the Archbishop of York: 'Every New Year is a time of hope; the darker our actual experience, the brighter the hope.' The lead writer concluded that at a very dark part of the war, 'our feet…are planted on the path that leads to victory.'

The biggest Christmas party was that at the South Reading Community Centre for evacuees. Reading Philanthropic Institution provided parcels to more than 600 poor families and hospital patients enjoyed the day even though blackout restrictions meant carols were sung by candlelight. There were no buses on 25 December and few cars ventured out, so for the first time in a year the roads were safe to cross.

Two couples tied the knot on Christmas Day: Harold Syrad and Marjorie Waite; and James Wise and Phyllis Clarke, who were married at Christ Church.

A final warning for the year was to keep mum! 'Blather begets blather.' The message was clear: don't talk to strangers.

It may have been a gloomy New Year but there were the January sales to look forward to. First off the mark was the Milward's Blue Pencil shoe sale commencing on 9 January.

CHAPTER THREE

1941

For those wanting a challenge in the New Year there was plenty of choice, from underwear machinists to van drivers to milk women – the successful candidate had to be smart and able to drive a horse. Among the standard jobs, such as experienced trouser machinist or experienced ledger clerk were some wartime only vacancies. Boys aged 16½ to 20 were wanted by the navy to train in the communications branch for the duration only. While wanting smart girls to train as 'nippys' and service counter hands, J. Lyons & Co wanted men over the age of 45 to act as firewatchers at their teashop. In competition, Box 1080 at *The Standard* wanted able-bodied men to act as Stirrup Pump Fire Fighters. Remuneration was 10s a shift from 6 pm to 8 am three to seven nights a week. Sleeping accommodation was provided. This was better pay than working for the NAAFI that wanted women for war work: a cook made just 24/9d a week. The Thames Valley Traction Company wanted women as drivers and conductresses. Female clerks aged 25 to 45 were needed by the Southern Railway but a male clerk, doing probably the same job, could be any age over 41.

There were many looking for work: a man over military age required a position, any responsibility; another desired full or part-time work as a shorthand typist, chauffeur, domestic work, anything. A Christian refugee wanted to be employed as a companion, help or housekeeper, as did an educated vegetarian refugee. Recently discharged from the army, an experienced salesman wanted a sound position. He was able to drive and

An imaginative advert to stop people wasting money on frivolous items and put it into National Savings instead.

possessed a 'thorough knowledge of provisions, cooked meats, etc., slight grocery'. The most intriguing was from a man who would consider working for a small salary: he was an Improver, Marcel waver and setter.

The Mayor in his New Year message hoped that 1941 would be a happy year, and after thanking the town for their efforts, he asked people to band together to defeat the Fire Bomb by having a watchful guard on every building and joining him in the Fire-Bomb Fighters' Corps.

He was right to worry. On 31 January it was estimated that 300 incendiary bombs were dropped on Reading during a late afternoon raid; but most caused no damage and 'what damage was caused was slight'. No fire spread 'thanks to the promptness of the firemen, ARP services and householders. Workmen, women in their homes, shoppers and children on their way home from school tackled the bombs with stirrup pumps, sand and earth. The damaged buildings included a church, shops, a garage and dwelling houses. In a number of houses, bedding was thrown out into the street by women, and in the houses where the occupiers were out, neighbours and friends broke into them and dealt with the fires.' One incendiary fell on the roof of a car which was turned on its side to get the bomb on the ground. Two high explosive bombs fell in open country causing a crater.

There was concern over flying glass from a bomb explosion. While it was sensible to protect windows with tape and with textile netting, it reduced stocks of material and provided sellers with a captive market, especially as it

Ex-Wilson Road schoolboy Lieutenant F. Green was in the news for being awarded the MBE.

was compulsory for businesses. One seller was Woolworth's who boasted they had stocks to meet any requirement. A week later they were telling night watchers to make sure their blackout was up to standard and naturally they could supply any materials needed.

Showing that even in times of adversity the British have a sense of humour, Milward's advertised their January sale with a topical reference: 'Haw-Haw [a Nazi news reader broadcasting to Britain] hasn't heard of it but – its news.' The blue pencil sale was good news and it would help save money.

Air raids were very much on people's minds. The government issued advice about how to get a good night's sleep in a public shelter, including tips on not snoring, what to do if you couldn't sleep, and not to wear too much clothing as shelters got hotter during the night.

Each issue carried a Roll of Honour. A French soldier, Gilbert Candelier, was reported as a PoW in France. His father was French and the family lived in Caversham. The first local to be named was Leading Signaller Norman Kirby who was presumed lost when the submarine he was serving on, HMS *Regulus,* failed to return. A week later the death of Sergeant-Pilot Leonard Hopgood of 50 Bourne Avenue was recorded as believed killed in action. But Sapper Ronald White of 108 Castle Street, who had been missing since May 1940, was reported safe and well.

Life continued as normally as it could. Reading Ramblers still rambled. People got married: a large number over the Christmas and New Year period. There were stray dogs in the police shelter and minor crimes were committed. Three Free French soldiers gave an undertaking to behave correctly and were let off; their crime was damaging a door and glass panel. A number of tradespeople were fined for defrauding the public: charging too much for an orange, and selling 28 lbs of margarine to someone without a permit and buying 28 lbs of margarine without a permit – two crimes for the price of one. Two youths aged 17, Edward Whitney of Henley Road and Gordon Absolom of Waverley Road, were charged with stealing a German Mauser and holster, and a cigarette case. Whether the owner of the gun had a licence was not mentioned.

There were few cases of drunkenness over Christmas and New Year. Only one made the news: a 19-year-old member of the ATS was so drunk she had to be taken to the police station for her own safety.

This quiet start contrasted with the Chief Constable's report to the Licensing Justices. There had been 'an increase in drunkenness of 50 per cent in 1940 as compared with the previous year', 75 compared to 51. Of these, 95 per cent were male and 67 per cent were non-residents. However, as the town's population had risen so much he felt the numbers were not entirely unsatisfactory. For the rest of the year the few reports of drunken behaviour were usually associated with a petty misdemeanour or occasionally theft. More unusual was the case of Thomas Buckland of 28 London Street. He was fined 10s and ordered to pay ambulance costs of 5s for being drunk while in charge of a pony and cart. Not only was he drunk but swore at the constable who wrote it all down. When shown the list of epithets he told the Bench that they were all wrong but then admitted he couldn't read. In his statement he said he had only had two drinks, but when arrested he was unable to stand without assistance.

Later in the year there was another story about a horse and cart. Mrs Rose Webb, an 87-year-old widow, was in her home, 1 George Street, when a horse and coal cart crashed through her front window. 'The whole of the large window frame was smashed in and the shafts of the lorry broke down surrounding brickwork. The horse came to a standstill inside the front parlour. The garden railings and the parlour wall were wrecked, leaving the interior of the parlour exposed to view. The driver of the lorry, Mr Henry East, of 40, Spring Gardens, Reading, was badly concussed and otherwise injured. He was given first-aid by Mrs. Webb before being conveyed to hospital.'

The story of how a 2½-year-old boy fell into the Thames chasing his balloon was particularly sad, and that of Mary Palmer equally so. She died from drinking spirits of salts (hydrochloric acid) thinking it might ease her stomach condition. The strange habit of hanging himself from all manner of things led to the death of 16-year-old Kenneth Francis of 927 Oxford Road. He had gone to the public lavatory in Oxford Road and after a half-hour wait was found hanging from a hook on the wall. Violet Main, a 20-year-old domestic servant at 53 London Road, died of severe burns from standing too close to an open fire, and Stanley Bradley of 40 The Mount walked into the trailer of a tractor and suffered compound fractures of the skull and a cerebral haemorrhage.

There were either fewer local conscientious objectors or it was no longer news: few reports had been printed since the second half of the previous year. However, three Reading men all claimed exemption: Leo Held of Wilson Road, Robert Hill of Oxford Road and Charles Buck of Blenheim Road. The first two were rejected, and Buck was told to do agricultural, ARP or AFS work but refused.

The first Patriotic Family to be featured were the five Bucklands on 24 January. Although not the biggest number so far, they did include two women, a nurse and a WAAF. One son was a sergeant in the Scots Guards, the other was an airman. The fifth was the father who had fought with the 1st Royal Berkshire Regiment in 1914 and re-joined the army in December 1939 at the age of about 45. In March they were joined by the Brooker Family of Field Road with five sons in the army. Competing for the title was the Allen family, who in April had five sons in the forces, two employed as firemen and a daughter engaged on war work.

There had been an obvious increase in the population. Very conservatively, the Registrar-General, in June, estimated a 24,000 increase on June 1939. In January Reading's population was stated as 100,600. The increase was the result of children compulsorily evacuated from London, voluntary evacuees who had left London with their families, the movement of some government departments from London making Reading a regional administrative centre, and the extra staff for the war industries as they expanded.

The official increase was almost certainly an underestimate, judging by the numbers attending Earley St. Peter's. Already

Evacuees attended local schools and continued their education. Here girls are being taught how to become housewives.

stretched by the increasing local population, it took refugee children from Battersea. In 1939 the school population was 294; the evacuees took the number to 535. Classes numbered up to 64 pupils because of teacher shortages.

Such a rapid increase in such a short time strained all the town's resources, and by October it was felt that the town was full. Reading became a 'Closed Town', one of the first in the country.

Some schools stayed open during school holidays for households with both parents working. Redlands was open on thirty-eight days during the summer holidays to cater for the children of war workers. Two years later a number of schools were designated play centres to cope with the increasing number of children. They were staffed by teachers who voluntarily gave up their holidays.

For others, the options for holidays were limited: seaside resorts were closed, transport was reduced, and families often did not have sufficient money. However, once the imminent danger of a German invasion had passed, things began to change.

Taking Woodley aerodrome as an example, it was not until the summer of 1941 that the management felt able to hold a holiday for employees. Whether it helped productivity is not recorded but it is noted that several hundred employees 'spent a rather alcoholic Sunday on a works outing to Brighton'.

In January and February, attendance at Reading schools was very poor because of measles, whooping cough and influenza.

Earlier in the war it had been realised that high power BBC transmitters would aid enemy navigation so it was decided that towns with populations of over 50,000 would receive a low powered transmitter to hear the Home Service. Reading's transmitter, Station 19, was housed inside the 'People's Pantry' and commenced broadcasting on 5 May 1941. Its position was felt by some as the reason for the 1943 bombing.

The 'People's Pantry' was a much greater success than anticipated and by February was serving 10-11,000 people a week. With that footfall it was fortunate the raiders came on early closing day.

The first air raid of the year was on Caversham, from St. Peter's Avenue to the borough boundary, and two bombs were dropped in Woodley. In the late afternoon of 30 January, raiders dropped around 300 incendiaries causing small fires, damage to over fifty properties, and injuring eight people. In the next raid, on 9 April, a number of incendiaries were dropped but little damage was caused. Reading was again an alternative target on the night of 10/11 April, but there were no casualties. It was the same on the night 3/4 May. On 9 May, Sutton's Trial Grounds were again visited by the Luftwaffe, and two days later a lone raider machine-gunned the gasworks damaging one gasholder and starting three minor fires.

There was still an expectation of the use of poison gas during raids and in the event of an invasion. Many respirators were over two years old and in need of repair, and growing children needed a new size. People were advised to take their gas mask to the Silver Street Instructional Centre for repair or exchange. This advice was followed by gas exercises in the town to motivate residents to carry their masks.

The loss of Sutton's Seeds records during a raid would have been a severe blow to the company. To protect them they moved the duplicates to the trial grounds in Earley where the building selected was reinforced against bomb blast. The company was also, like everyone else, affected by the paper shortage. They only sent out catalogues if they were requested on a postcard handed out by one of their sales team.

Huntley & Palmers had also taken measures. They had asked their bank to keep sufficient cash to make up a week's wages at short notice, and stored debtors details safely along with other essential documents. To keep an exact record of the 400 types and weights of biscuits produced before the war, samples of each were sealed in airtight tins for reference.

As with the very young, one type of gasmask did not suit or fit everyone. This respirator was designed for people with facial deformities or throat trouble. It was issued by the Health Department on the production of a form completed by a doctor.

In January the Ministry of Food sanctioned a release of sugar and boiled sweets, and then from October children could purchase a meal at school. A horse and cart brought the meals to each school from the central kitchen in Southampton Street. Sometimes it was difficult to find a place to eat, in schools already using every room and more for classes. For those willing to pay, milk was available at ½d a small bottle; it was not free until after the war.

In June clothing was rationed. Each person was provided with coupons to buy one complete outfit a year. Children, because they grew out of clothes, were provided with ten more than an adult. It didn't include compulsory school uniform. To make a scarce resource go further, dressmaking classes were held in homes. 'Make do and mend' was a fruitful way

Henry Ford and his son Edsel donated these emergency food vans to the County Borough. Other towns and cities benefited from their generosity: a total of 350 were donated to Britain.

Boys were also taught how to cook, well, cakes at least. These evacuee children are being taught how to make a cocoanut (sic) cake at Newtown School.

of extending the life of a garment or using the good pieces to make a new item.

After the fighting in France the Royal Berkshire Regiment had been sending clothing and food parcels to those taken prisoner. The fighting in North Africa had increased the number to such an extent they were no longer able to provide comforts to those serving as well as those in captivity. The latter took priority. The *China Dragon* asked serving and ex-soldiers to donate woollen goods and to keep worn-out woollens for reuse. Pleased with their efforts they sent the Red Cross 1,033 pairs of socks, 381 helmets, 305 scarves, 300 mittens, 226 pullovers, 99 gloves, 44 wristlets, six shirts, and three pairs of pyjamas to men of the regiment.

Francis Hartley of 2 Edgehill Street was a Dunkirk casualty; his death was assumed a year later. He was a territorial in the Gloucestershire Regiment.

Collecting waste material had been a priority in 1940. However, early in the year the townspeople were admonished for their flagging interest: research showed that only 12 of 100 houses sampled were saving waste. The Borough Surveyor appealed to householders not to put useful articles in the dustbin, especially paper. This was followed by an advert detailing exactly what was needed and how to deal with it for collection. As now, not all types of paper were recyclable and as food waste went to chickens and pigs many things we recycle today for composting, like tea leaves and citrus fruit skins, were unsuitable. The figures for December were nearly 52 tons of paper, 45 tons 17 cwt of kitchen waste and over seven tons of bones recycled along with nearly two tons of textiles and 3¾ tons of glass. Ferrous metal was a disappointment at under 1½ tons.

Gilbert Candelier, a French national living in Caversham, was reported as a PoW in France. He was serving in the French Army; his step-brother was serving in the British Army.

No one could complain about the town's rate of saving. In 1940 it had averaged £42,738 a week, saving £3,068,409 in total and in 1941 was averaging over £50,000. As usual further effort was wanted.

Digging for Victory as a slogan had been around since the start of the war, but research had shown that for many it was meaningless; after all, food production was for farmers. To raise awareness of the need for people to supplement their vegetables by growing their own, Reading ran its first 'Dig for Victory' week.

They were especially appealing to the estimated 60,000 evacuees in the town to get involved. The campaign emphasised Germany's intention to starve the country out of the war by sinking ships. Producing more crops would help win the war by releasing space for other cargoes. If that was not enough to make people want an allotment, then there was a financial incentive. A novice allotment holder off the Wokingham Road kept accounts: despite some crop failures due to drought and other reasons he showed a net profit for 1940 of £5 3s (around £250 in 2019 prices). The message was clear: it paid in cash, in kind, in more appetising food, and in healthy exercise of mind and body and it would help hasten the end of the war.

To help the housewife make the most of the ingredients available, the Ministry of Food set up Food Advice Centres across the country. On 14 March, the Reading centre opened in Cross Street. There were demonstrations, and trained specialists to answer questions and provide tips on anything to do with food.

Another female contingent marching in the parade was the Women's Land Army, seen here following a tractor.

Food Week followed, opened by J.B. Priestley, during which a series of events told of the 'necessity for the most economic and proper use of food'. There were experts on hand to give advice, and prizes for cookery ideas.

One suggestion was to keep rabbits because one tame doe was estimated to produce '90lb. of wholesome palatable flesh annually in exchange for grass, garden wastage, hay and a few potatoes'. If 100,000 households kept just one doe it would provide '4,000 tons of flesh, 3,000,000 skins and 10,000 tons of garden manure annually'. Concluding in words that would not be penned today, when the time came 'for the selected ones to make the great sacrifice, they will make it uncomplainingly and with the knowledge, so to speak, that in due course the little ones they have left behind will emulate the parental example'.

Submarine warfare also meant a shortage of seed for pet birds. To stop the wholesale slaughter of cage birds, the PDSA and Dumb Friends produced a range of leaflets with alternative foods. Food was not a problem for cat and dog owners, as the Dog's Dinner at 290 Oxford Road advertised an unlimited supply of unrationed meat for pets. For those who would part with their pets for the duration, the War Office was appealing for dogs for war work.

A paper salvage campaign office was opened in Reading, with window displays showing how paper collected could become war material. One ton could become: 140,000 cups for fuses, 70,000 engine gaskets, 70,000 machine gun targets, or 4,000 square feet of wall board for temporary buildings; the list was seemingly endless. A simple demonstration explained how quickly a ton could be collected: 600 copies of *The Times* weighed one cwt. Special collections of waste paper – newspapers, magazines, periodicals, and music – took place during the fortnight 21 April–3 May. It was to be a countrywide campaign and Reading had been selected as the first town.

The government needed volunteers for war work and wanted people to register at their local office of the Ministry of Labour and National Service. To increase interest in munitions work, 3 to 16 August were designated as Reading Women's War Work Week. Like many fundraising drives that lasted a week but continued until the target was reached, this opened on a Sunday and closed two weeks later on a Saturday. Reading's women were told their duty was war work. Shortly afterwards, in the properties wanted, an unidentified company asked for an industrial type property with vacant possession suitable for work of NATIONAL IMPORTANCE. The importance of the work was emphasised in October by a visit from Ernest Bevin, Minister of Labour and National Service, who appealed to men and women to put their 'last ounce' of energy into the production of armaments.

Money was always needed: for Greece, for Malta, to buy a Spitfire, from women whose name began with a V to support the V Spitfire Fund or at home to help provide guide dogs for blinded soldiers. Men were also needed: the Reading Battalion of the Home Guard had places to fill.

For those not giving their time or wanting to work in munitions, there was an alternative: National Savings Stamps. Available at 6d or 2s 6d they could be used to make deposits in the Post Office or TSB or to buy National Savings Certificates of Defence Bonds. The motto was 'Work, Save, Lend today and everyday till victory is achieved'.

During Women's War Week, this flag was carried through the streets on a Bren Carrier. It was captured by a Reading soldier during the Lofoten Islands raid on 3/4 March 1941.

The request to save was constant. Even without official campaigns there was always a smaller version, like Reading's Summer Campaign, which ran from 1 August until 31 October. Savings groups were set up, each with the aim of saving for

As part of Women's War Work Week, there was a large parade through the town. Included in the display were tanks and a considerable number of marching women: WAAFs who were evidently cheered by the crowds.

The National Savings ladder from the previous year was brought out for Warship Week to show progress towards the target. The Mayor is pointing out that the town had exceeded the target by £171,926.

specific items. One group aimed to save £1,000 to buy a barrage balloon and small ambulance. Most were more modest, saving for machine guns or bombs. Huntley & Palmers target of £3,000 for five heavy ambulances was £4,200 by the end of September, enough for seven. Similarly, MacFisheries' aim to buy 12 parachutes at £480 was reached with enough to buy 13¾.

There was little subtlety when it came to raising money. On 22 August a tank column made a two-day visit to the town, starting at War Memorial Square. There were demonstrations

In August 1941, a tank column visited the town to initiate a new fund, this time for tanks. The tanks were parked at the Forbury to allow the public to get a good view. They were named Bashful, Dopey, Grumpy and Happy.

on Hill's Meadow, with a programme of visits to the major employers in the town. The tanks, painted with the names of Snow White dwarfs – Bashful, Dopey, Grumpy and Happy – were on display across the town for the public to inspect. The bottom line was money.

Following the Spitfire Fund, Reading started a Tank Fund. With the fund barely started, there was a Flag Day on 30 August, this time for the National Air Raid Distress Fund. The target was £1,000 but less than £900 had been raised by its closing date. As with other appeals it was kept open until the total was reached in mid-September.

The tanks were very popular, especially as the public was allowed to climb all over them. No chance of doing this in twenty-first century Britain.

As a thank you for buying a Spitfire, the town received 'an artistic plaque of white metal mounted on white oak' to stand on a table or desk. Under RAF wings it read:

In the Hour of Peril
People of Reading
Earned the Gratitude
Of the British Nations
Sustaining the Valour of
The Royal Air Force
And Fortifying the Cause
Of Freedom
By the Gift of Spitfire Aircraft
They Shall Mount up With Wings as Eagles.

Gunner R. Friend was reported missing in June during the fighting in North Africa but was later reported as a PoW. At the same time, his brother, Sergeant Harold Friend, was reported missing on operations. He also turned up later as a PoW.

Hundreds of Reading workers contributed to the Penny-a-week collection. Across the country, five million contributors raised a £1,000,000 a year. There was also an appeal for volunteers prepared to collect the money, door-to-door, every week until the end of the war.

Economy was key. The Post Office provided advice to reduce waste: 'use one stamp instead of two.' Thames Valley Traction Co, the local bus company, wanted residents to 'travel between the hours of 9.30 am and 12.30 pm or 2.30 & 4 pm' to reduce the pressure at rush hour. In September, bus services were curtailed to save fuel with the last public transport at 9.30 instead of 10.15 pm.

As in the last war there was a Comforts Depot. At a reception in the Jacobean Restaurant, Mrs Green, the depot organiser, told the guests that across Berkshire there were over 300 registered knitters who in a year had completed 14,000 garments for the armed forces. The depot also received many gifts of books, cards, gramophones and records, and many other items which were sent to the troops. In late October there was a request for spare small pianos for the troops in Iceland.

In March, the Chief Constable reported on traffic accidents and crime. There had been a large increase in juvenile crime, much carried out by evacuees. However, there had been a dramatic downturn in burglary/housebreaking and a small decrease in shoplifting. In 1940, 86 people across Berkshire had died as a result of a road accident compared with 60 the previous year. This was countered by a small fall in the number injured: 15 fewer.

There were a number of sad stories published during the war about babies. The first was in May. A parcel floating down the Thames contained the body of a male child wrapped in two pieces of white cloth with a piece of wood attached to its back by a piece of string. There were no signs of violence. The coroner estimated death as three days previous, and recorded an open verdict, saying that death was due to lack of attention at birth. In mid-September, a male child, this time alive, was found in the Abbey ruins. The three week old boy was in good health and well-dressed. Apart from the clothing and blanket he was wrapped in, there were no clues.

The sinking of the battleship HMS *Hood* was a national disaster. Aboard were two Reading men, both reported missing: gunner

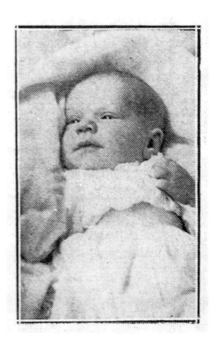

The baby found in a phone box: parents unknown.

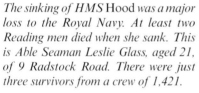
The sinking of HMS Hood *was a major loss to the Royal Navy. At least two Reading men died when she sank. This is Able Seaman Leslie Glass, aged 21, of 9 Radstock Road. There were just three survivors from a crew of 1,421.*

Royal Marine Corporal Reginald Mills, aged 24, of 141 Caversham Road, was killed fighting in Crete. He is commemorated on the Plymouth Naval Memorial.

Arthur Cox, aged 18, of 307 Northumberland Avenue, and Able Seaman Leslie Glass, aged 21, of 9 Radstock Road.

Between April and June local rivers claimed the lives of Private Reginald Smith, 8-year-old Alan Gale, John Skipper, a retired traveller, 15-year-old Anthony Duffin, and 19-year-old Frederick Catchpole. One was a suicide, the others accidents. In February the Kennet failed to claim an attempted suicide: Constable Horace Smith, pausing only to take off his overcoat, dived in and pulled the lady out, for which he was officially commended.

In July, a miracle was reported in the town. Mrs Pearcey of 146 Bath Road regained her sight. During the Great War, while working on munitions, she 'lost an eye through a splinter flying into it'. After a brain operation she lost the sight of her remaining eye leaving her totally blind for eight years. She fell off a chair when blacking out a window and, feeling very tired, went to bed. In the morning she could see everything.

Although the likelihood of a major aerial attack was small, the ARP still had to be prepared. At the end of July, they and other services held a large-scale exercise in and around the borough. As well as noise and disturbance, the public were warned that tear gas might be used.

According to the paper it was a convincing exercise that included 'all the incidents of a real invasion'. The combined military and civil defence exercise at the end of July was intended to test the Home Guard that was defending the town from a four-pronged attack during which the quantity of tear gas released

At the end of July the civil defence and military held a full scale exercise which included low-flying planes and mock bombs. This shows a trolley bus being bombed in Broad Street.

Further realism to the exercise was added by rescuing casualties under difficult conditions and having gas casualties waiting for treatment.

was sufficient for it to be felt in Earley. Planes dive-bombed the town releasing 300 'incendiary bombs', troops were transported by air and dummies were placed in fields to represent parachute invaders. The attack commenced at 5.45 am and by 8 am the enemy were at the railway stations having crossed the Thames using Caversham and Reading Bridges. To make it more realistic a number of people posed as Fifth Columnists with the police checking everyone's identity cards.

This was followed a month later by another exercise but this time without the armed forces. It was held on a Sunday morning during which fifty-two incidents were staged, including unexploded bombs, casualties, imaginary fires and craters in roads. Casualties were rescued from upper storeys of buildings and from beneath wreckage with realistic sound effects including the whistle of bombs falling. The Oxford Road was blocked by unexploded bombs, casualties were treated and then taken to hospital, and a harmless gas was released for decontamination squads to deal with. Emergency food and rest centres were opened and practised their role during the exercise.

Earlier in the year Princess Helena Victoria had visited the town, at the end of July the King and Queen visited Bearwood

Merchant Navy School. At the school were 200 boys and 100 girls – orphans of merchant seamen. The boys were training for service with the merchant fleets; a few days later the King inspected the local Home Guard.

During the year there were constant call-ups, and by August men born in 1897 were registered, many of whom had fought in the Great War. Normally, because of the National Registration the authorities knew who to send for. However, in July they sent for their youngest recruit, certainly an administrative error. Mr and Mrs Sidwell of 82 Queen's Road received an official letter asking their daughter to attend for an interview to register for employment. It was correctly addressed but 17 years early: she was only 11 months old at the time.

Men were needed for Civil Defence. In September all British male subjects between the ages of 18 and 60, unless exempted, like lunatics, doctors, policemen or mariners, were deemed to have enrolled for civil defence duty. The youngest were enrolled first.

Queuing was a constant problem and sometimes behaviour was so poor people ended up in court. Walter Morris of 22 Lower Armour Road was summoned for failing to produce his identity card, assaulting (kicking) George Green, a corporation official regulating the queue for the Bear Inn bus in Broad Street and endeavouring to enter a trolley vehicle before other persons standing in the queue in front of him. He was fined 10s for failing to produce his identity card, £1 for the assault, and 10s for attempting to enter a bus out of turn. It was not just the public who were at fault. There were also complaints about bus and trolley staff who did not stop at recognised stops.

Each week newly released books were reviewed in the papers; the selection was wide and eclectic. One was *The Sayings of Muhammad*. The reviewer noted that because of centuries of prejudice, only a small section of the Western World understood the breadth and scope behind the teachings of the Prophet. He then suggested, presciently, that 'we shall be wise to learn all we can of the prime moral guidance of millions' especially because at the time of writing, Muslims were fighting with and for us.

Quite how this happened was not explained: a trolley bus collided with the brickwork and railings of a bridge in Southampton Street.

In the first case of its kind in Reading, Fire Watcher Sidney Gaines, of Crescent Road, was fined £5. The crime was not turning up for his shift he had allotted himself as the chief fire guard for the area. His reason for being absent was that he felt it was his duty to be at home with his wife and children in the event of an alert.

Among the stories of brave men and their medals was that of a Scout. On 19 June, 14-year-old Peter Clifford 'rescued a 7-year-old girl from drowning by diving into the swirling waters just below Caversham Weir. After bringing the child to the bank in an unconscious condition, Clifford brought his scout training into play by successfully applying artificial respiration.' For this he was awarded the gilt cross, a Scout Association award for gallantry, together with a certificate recording the deed.

During a civil defence demonstration, women members pose with their trailer pump.

Good news in October was an allocation of oranges to Berkshire, but they were not for everyone. Only children under six were to receive an allotment of 1 lb of fresh oranges.

Frances Braithwaite, aged 18 months, did not receive her oranges. She was dead. In the most serious case of the year at the Berkshire Assizes in Reading, her mother and father were charged with her death. They were found guilty by the jury of manslaughter and the husband sentenced to five years; his wife's sentence was deferred pending enquiries about her mental state.

The hope was once again to beat the 1940 collection. Even before the collection money from churches was in, the 1940 total had been beaten by £433 18s 6d with £2,582 19s raised by the sale of poppies and wreaths alone. Putting this in the context of house prices at the time, at auction during the summer, houses in Cardiff Road fetched between £150 (number 23) and £230 (number 1).

At the same time preparations were being made for another fund raising event: Warships Week, in March 1942, with a target of £1,200,000, an increase on the successful War Weapons Week total of £851,000. The committee noted that 'a great effort will be needed'.

At the express wish of the King, once again there was no formal Armistice Day service. But this did not stop ex-servicemen's organisations or other bodies placing wreaths on the memorial as long as the Chief Constable was consulted beforehand. A number of churches held short services of remembrance on Tuesday, 11 November.

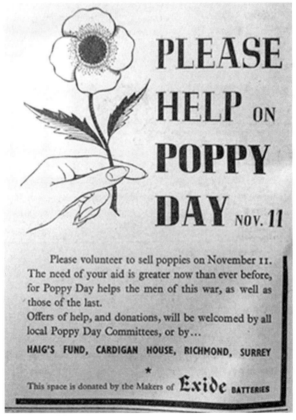

As with today's programmes on television, adverts for important causes during the war were often sponsored by other organisations. An advert for Poppy sales sponsored by Exide batteries.

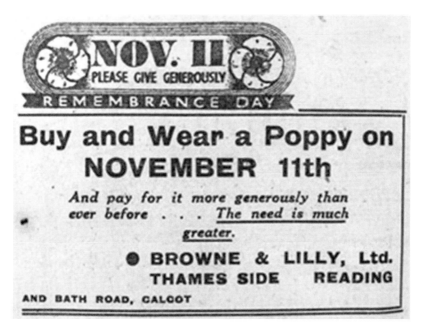

Advertising sponsored by Browne & Lilly, to encourage the purchase of poppies.

As ever, the message from the Post Office was to post early and preferably before noon. The message from the Reading Philanthropic Institution was the same as when they had been inaugurated in 1910: they asked for donations of food and clothing to help the poor. The Mayor launched his annual appeal which bolstered the work of the Philanthropists. The Reading Chamber of Commerce again recommended that all shops, other than food stores, close on Christmas Day (Thursday), Friday and Sunday.

The leader writer of *The Standard* told readers, in case they hadn't noticed it, that 'Christmas this year, as last, must necessarily be kept in a subdued mood' but for the children's sake try and make the occasion as cheerful as possible. Many evacuees went home over the period and were not expected to return if the lull in the bombing continued.

In the week before Christmas, the paper carried news about four local men. Three were reported dead and one missing. Marine Edward Woodman of 461 Basingstoke Road, Gunner

Leslie Johnson of Langley Hill, and Marine N. Wheeler of Emmer Green were listed as killed in action. Private R. Herbert of 50 Bedford Road was officially listed as missing as nothing had been heard from him since October last.

As Boxing Day was a Friday, *The Standard* printed on Wednesday, Christmas Eve. It also carried a Roll of Honour: A.C.1 Bruce Ferguson of Eastern Avenue was reported as presumed killed and Pilot Gerald Grigg of the Spreadeagle Hotel, Norfolk Road, was reported missing. In the next columns were reports of local weddings and a Golden Wedding Anniversary.

To aid the Christmas cheer there was again no shortage of alcohol. There were also concerts to attend like that performed by the Red Cross massed bands. In the cinemas there was a wide range of films, and for those wishing to dance there were plenty to choose from. Huntley & Palmer's party provided tea,

Often on the same page as the deaths and casualties were those rewarded for their achievements. Corporal Edward Carpenter, RAFVR, of Cherry Cot, Old Bath Road, was mentioned in despatches. He survived the war.

Sergeant Pilot Gerald Grigg was reported missing on operations. His death was later confirmed as 11 December 1941, serving with 35 Squadron flying Halifax bombers.

a film and a variety performance by Walter Lenham, a radio entertainer, for 250 children.

Once again, the vicar of Sonning felt unable to wish his parishioners a merry Christmas but did wish them every blessing. 'This great Festival with its message of peace and goodwill comes home to us more than ever in the stern days through which we are passing.' The Mayor was more upbeat: 'My wish,' he wrote, 'of a happy Christmas to all Reading people, everywhere, is one which I hope will echo right throughout the coming year.'

There was no stopping the Savings Executive. Just days before Christmas they held a special meeting to plan the various subcommittees needed for Warship Week. The plan was to be discussed at 3 pm on 9 January.

Make this a SAVINGS-GIFT CHRISTMAS

Send everyone the colourful card that combines greetings with a practical, patriotic gift that helps the country as well as your friends. Get your cards now and fix on as many stamps as you can, ready to send out in good time for Christmas. Cards are FREE to purchasers of Savings Stamps — from Post Offices, Trustee Savings Banks, Savings Groups and Centres or Honorary Official Agents. *Ask also about National Savings Gift Tokens in units of 15/- up to any amount.*

ISSUED BY THE NATIONAL SAVINGS COMMITTEE

Frivolous purchases at Christmas were frowned upon and the best present was a Christmas card from the National Savings Committee (free) in which to stick the best present – savings stamps.

Able Seaman George Wicks was 20 when he was killed on active service while serving on HMS Galatea. It was torpedoed in the Mediterranean on 14 December 1941 with the loss of 469 of her crew. He had been in the navy for five years.

As the pool of available manpower was rapidly being drained, many Reading men suddenly found their reserved occupation had become unreserved. There was only a short time in which to decide what to do and the RAF were quick to capitalise on it. They wanted unreserved men aged under 33 to volunteer for flying duties. Their office was at St. Giles's School, London Road.

Before enlisting there was still time to enjoy the New Year. People were spoiled for choice at the Olympia with a dance every day from 24 December to 3 January except Christmas Day and Sunday the 29th. On 31 December there was a New Year's Eve Ball at Queen Anne's School, and on 2 January Reading Rambling Club joined in the festivities with a dance in aid of the Red Cross Fund.

The Co-op thanked customers for their forbearance during a difficult year. It did not give Christmas greetings; instead it gave a wish for the New Year: 1942 ANNUS MIRABILIS!! Year of Wonders, Wonderful Year, and one they hoped would be a climb to Victory and Peace.

CHAPTER FOUR

1942

The Mayor's New Year message was advice given by the Bishop of Lincoln: 'Go bravely on doing the daily duties and trusting that as the day is, so shall our strength be.'

The Standard opened the year with lists of Christmas weddings complete with details of attendees and the wedding dresses. The same page also contained the Roll of Honour which included Chief Petty Officer Gordon Johnson of Pitts Lane, Earley, and reports of two missing RAF men, Sergeant Clark of Northumberland Avenue and Sergeant Webb of Cressingham Road. Each week there was a new list of names, many with photographs.

Such reports continued throughout the war. The vicar of Tywford and Ruscombe received the news of his eldest son's death in Malta; Wing Commander John Dowland had won the George Cross for his bravery in defusing bombs earlier in the war. Parents remembered their sons in the deaths columns although not as frequently as the previous war. A typical example was: Kirk. – To the dear memory of my darling boy, Sergt. Lewis John Kirk, RAFVR, March 21, 1941. *Per ardua ad astra.*

There was also news about the injured. With Japan now an enemy, the Far East had suddenly become an active military area. An early report concerned Maurice Boylett of Hatherley Road, serving in the RAF in Singapore; he had been seriously injured in an air raid. Dr and Mrs Falconer of Tywford received news that both their sons were missing, one in Hong Kong, the other in Singapore. Not all the news from the Far East was

With the ever increasing demand for men by the forces, women, as during the Great War, took their place. Here they are acting as rail porters.

correct. Wireless operator Kenneth Martin had been evacuated from Singapore and was safe, and signalman N. Williams of 10, Council Cottages, Shinfield, who had been reported missing in Malaya had turned up safe and sound in Africa. Finding out that a loved one was a PoW was a relief at the time, but it was not known that Japanese captives would be treated so badly and not all would return.

Back home, Dennis Carter disappeared on Christmas Day morning and naturally his wife and relatives were keen to know his whereabouts. Whether he was found or not is unknown. Flight Lieutenant Pickering of St George's Road was buried in Wales; Private Carey of Newtown died in an accident.

Mrs Gardner of Cranbury Road, aged 87, became a great-great-grandmother in February. The Duchess of Kent visited the Reading Hospital Supply Depot. William Cope was

This is the YMCA Information Bureau, Station Yard, which aided travellers passing through Reading.

awarded the Royal Humane Society's parchment for gallantry for saving a 4-year-old boy from drowning in the Kennet. Two brothers, Corporal F. Wilsher and Sergeant H. Wilsher of Whitley met up in the Middle East while on leave. Charles Crowe of Dorset Street was reported safe after his ship sank in the Mediterranean. The parents of Harold Pickering and Robert Wickens received positive news after their sons were reported missing – both were now PoWs. And in March, Reading opened its first British Restaurant at the Oxford Hall, Oxford Road. It was similar to the People's Pantry and allowed residents to buy a meal for a shilling; a desert and drink cost another tuppence.

In August, *The Standard* reported the amazing story of NAAFI manager J. Haddy of Culver Road. He survived the bombing of his ship by wearing a gasmask. During the attack he was blown off his feet in a fume-filled compartment that was filling with oil and water. To protect himself from the fumes he put on his gasmask, and with difficulty managed to climb up a deck. After closing the manhole below and closing another hatch he lost consciousness. Five hours later he found himself on the upper deck. The rescue parties had noticed a floating respirator, which on being pulled out had a body attached. Seemingly dead he was laid out and one of the NAAFI staff noticed he was still breathing. After being cleaned up, apart from leg wounds he was found to be in good health.

In August there were stories from the carrier HMS *Eagle*. Three men from Reading serving on her all survived; two were brothers, one of whom had never swum before. Mr C. Bowen gave a thrilling talk on his rescue from the liner *Athenia* and at Christmas the Reading Rotary Club heard the tale of an escapee from Guernsey.

The government decided that everyone needed a holiday at Whitsun but did not provide extra trains; they were for the military first. The government wanted holidays to be taken at home: a 'Staycation'. Reading put together a long programme of events, starting at the end of June, to keep people occupied, relaxed and happy. The first event, on 27 June, was a gathering on the river promenade. It was estimated that 1,500 joined in the day, with hundreds dancing in a specially prepared arena. Families picnicked, and the British Restaurant's marquee was kept busy all day. The river was crowded with boats, punts and dinghies. Music was provided by Miss Marie Hyde and her accordion band. A holidays-at-home bureau opened in King's Road with information about future events which included sports competitions, a darts tournament, tennis tournaments, bowls matches, musical events, cycle trips, swimming and river sports, flower shows and concerts at the Olympia. A highlight of the programme for late August was 'a display of all forms of fire-fighting, from the old days when hand drawn manuals and leather buckets were used, down to the present-day methods of dealing with blitz conditions.'

The 'Staycation' was invented in the Second World War. With many beaches closed and limited space on trains to get to the sea front, it was easier to stay at home and participate in the many events on offer.

Events were planned to last ten weeks and naturally there were amusements and activities for those under 18: free swimming, sand pits, free use of pitches in parks, Punch and Judy shows, decorated bicycle competitions, fishing competitions, pony rides,

Two summer weddings (both at Christ Church) chosen from the many in the papers: Pilot Officer T. Bartlett and Miss Grace Phillips (left) and Private T. Humphries and Miss Gladys Dolton. All survived the war.

swings, roundabouts and other amusements on the promenade. The museum welcomed children, especially supervised small parties. The message was simple: 'If your journey is not essential – DO NOT TRAVEL.'

Days into the New Year there were cuts in rations: firstly to sugar and butter allowances, and then a halving of the cheese ration from 9 February. The same day, soap – but not shaving soap, dental soaps, shampoo powders, liquid soap, or scourers – was rationed.

Worse for many was the disappearance of white bread; it was replaced by the National Loaf made from 85 per cent British flour, thereby saving shipping space. Before its appearance the loaf's colour was kept secret, the public being told it was good pure bread and they would get used to its colour. It was not popular and was known by many as Hitler's Secret Weapon.

There was no water shortage but residents were asked to use less because pumping it used fuel. To further save fuel, people were asked to carry their shopping home; delivery services were being reduced or discontinued. Although tiresome, it meant more petrol, rubber and manpower were available for the war effort. The soft drinks manufacturer Corona apologised for the disruption emphasising that its products could still be bought from local retailers. An investigation had shown that thirty-one different companies were delivering bread to the same street; deliveries were rationalised with bread not necessarily coming from the household's usual baker.

To reduce fuel consumption, people were asked to 'Switch it off, Turn it out, Cut it down, Do without.' With cold weather coming, people were also asked to spare the poker: anything that made the fire burn faster was an act of sabotage.

Paper became so scarce that it became an offence to waste it. The penalty was serious: £100 or three months imprisonment or both; on indictment before a higher court it was £500 or two years or both. To reinforce the need to save paper there was a regular waste paper quiz in the press with such tricky questions as 'What do I do with greasy paper as it is no use for salvage?' Answer: use it to light fires.

The shortage of rubber was so desperate the government was willing to pay for it. In 1940 metal put out for salvage had been stolen and then sold to scrapyards; now an eagle-eyed thief had stolen a large deflated rubber ball from the doorstep of Highfield in Elm Lane. The indignant householder wrote to the papers saying he would not put out his rubber hot water bottles unless someone called to collect them.

D.F.M. FOR READING MAN

Sergt.-Wireless-operator-Air-gunner Frederick Leonard Dolton, son of Mr. and Mrs. F. Dolton, of 25, St. Edward's Road, Reading, has been awarded the Distinguished Flying Medal.

Twenty-four years of age, Sergt. Dolton joined the R.A.F. at the age of 19. He was educated at Alfred Sutton School and was a keen member of the St. Luke's Church Lads Brigade. Sergt. Dolton is married, his wife residing at Gloucester.

Sergeant Dolton, a wireless operator air gunner, who before marrying had lived at 25 St. Edward's Road, was in the paper for his award of the DFM. He survived the war.

The capture of the rubber tree plantations by the Japanese made it a very valuable commodity. Fortunately it was recyclable, and as a result of the rubber salvage drive, large quantities of rubber balls and water bottles were handed in to be made into war materials such as tyres, as this cartoon shows.

As well as returning scarce milk bottles and jam jars, housewives were asked to bag dry clean rags for collection. They could be turned into clothing, paper, roofing felt and new wiping rags for engines and machinery. Even old toothpaste tubes were wanted; they were made of metal. The jam jars were needed by fruit preservation centres, which bought surplus local fruit to make into jam.

June saw yet another salvage campaign. The Mayor opened an exhibition in Heelas' store front devoted to how household waste could be turned into useful materials for the war effort. In the store were 100 photographs showing the making of munitions. Joining in the fun, Reading Council designated 2 July as Corporation Salvage Day, when heads of department were able to decide what was salvage and what should kept. Each department went through every cupboard, corner, drawer, shelf and any other receptacle in search of old reference books, documents, bills, receipts, note blocks and anything else deemed not worth keeping. As the town's businesses were expected to do the same, it is easy to see why there are many gaps in records from this period.

Books were high on the list of valuable salvage. While the intention was good – paper was scarce – it had not been thought through and many rare and valuable books went for salvage. At the same time as tens of thousands of books were being pulped, the armed forces and Red Cross were asking for book donations. *The Standard* put the importance of paper into a simple context. If everyone who went to the cinema in a week – about 20 million people – recycled their ticket, it would make enough cardboard for 30,000 Red Cross boxes for PoWs.

Wokingham District Council was proud of its efforts, providing monthly totals for paper, rags, bones, bottles, jars, metals and rubber. In July it raised over £450 from salvage, with most coming from paper. Berkshire was also proud of its effort during the June/July salvage week; it had gathered 1,446 tons 15 cwt, and like Wokingham the greatest weight was paper. When tonnage was compared with population, per thousand inhabitants Reading was an easy winner with 5.04 tons to a Berkshire total of 3.30 tons. One suggestion to increase the amount of scrap metal in the collection was to melt down street lamps that no longer served a purpose.

The Brewers' Society reiterated the advice to keep rabbits, although they calculated one doe could provide 45lbs of meat annually compared with the government's 90lbs. For those with more space and uncomplaining neighbours, pigs and/or poultry could be kept to provide meat. Providing food for them that was not rationed was lucrative at £4 10s a ton with free delivery. Alternatively, and easier, Brooke Bond suggested that buying their beef cubes would make the ration go further.

Every week the papers carried court reports. A Londoner, Howard Austin was charged with unlawfully wearing a naval uniform. William Bullock from the Oxford Road pleaded guilty to wearing a naval officer's uniform. Gunner Bull was sentenced to three months imprisonment for stealing bikes and Aaron Smith of Northumberland Avenue was found guilty of receiving the stolen bikes. The company J.M. Stone in Market Place was fined £50 with 15 guineas costs for selling a wireless valve in excess of the price regulations while Frederick Naish was sentenced to one month's hard labour for receiving eleven gallons of stolen petrol. The magistrate was probably correct in sending 17-year-old Douglas Cousins for medical tests. He was charged with stating he was a member of the Secret Service and that he had been parachuted into the country from enemy territory; he had previously impersonated a Home Guard officer. When he promised not to be foolish again his case was dismissed on payment of 4s.

Women appeared regularly before the Bench, usually but not always for theft. Kathleen Morgan of Westfield Road was sentenced to six months imprisonment for stealing the clothes of an evacuee who had been billeted with her and since gone back to London. Instead of returning his clothing she had pawned some and converted others to her own use. Gwen Andrews and Margaret Heath of Chapel Hill were summoned and convicted of assault; they had kicked, beaten and used abusive language towards Rita Richardson also of Chapel Hill.

Another sign of the times was the severity of some of the sentences handed out. In April a mother of seven was sent to prison for shoplifting and Charles Fuller was sentenced to one month's imprisonment for breaking a shop window. Sidney Thomas, who already had a long list of previous convictions, was sentenced to three years' penal servitude for breaking and entering three houses. Charles Fuller, of no fixed abode, was sent to prison for a month for lodging in the open air, a crime he had committed before.

Such was total war that being late for work or taking time off without good reason was a crime under the Defence Regulations. In November, Elsie Green of Great Knollys Street pleaded guilty to being persistently late for work and two counts of being absent from work without reasonable excuse. She had been warned numerous times but had persisted with her behaviour. As she was only 18 she was not sent to prison or fined the £300 she could have been. She promised to be prompt for work and asked to be released to join the services.

The courts also dealt with marital problems. Typical cases were that of Arthur Smith and Sergeant Allen: both were granted a decree nisi on the grounds of their wife's adultery. Later in the year Arthur Connolly of Bath Road was granted a divorce: his wife had committed adultery just weeks after they had got married.

In Woodley, the proprietor, and his daughter, of the Glow-worm Club were fined for supplying intoxicating liquor outside permitted hours and the club closed for a year. At the same time, the Chief Constable reported that this was just one of the two clubs struck off and that the remaining forty-one had behaved correctly. Neither was he concerned about the number of prosecutions for drunkenness, 84 against 78 in the previous year, because 59 were visitors. The statistics showed the worst months for drunkenness were January, April and August and the worst days were Mondays, Tuesdays, Wednesdays and Saturdays. Edward Cleere of Highgrove Terrace was fined for riding a cycle on a Sunday while drunk and without lights. He had been to a wedding and could not resist the temptation of a bike ride.

Three months later, the Chief Constable was pleased to report that overall there had been only a small rise in crime in the town. However, there had been a considerable increase in probation.

In his June report, comparing road traffic accidents, nine more people had died on the road and 183 more injured than in 1940. Compared with 1941, there was a decrease of six persons killed and 163 injured.

The Medical Officer reported an increase in TB cases and concomitant higher death rate compared with 1941. He blamed this on a higher population, war fatigue and extremely cold winters. Bovine infection was also a problem. With the scheduled demolition of the TB dispensary and no replacement planned, and mass radiography not feasible, it was an ongoing problem.

Flushed with the success of buying a Spitfire and having money left over, it was decided to buy another. By 2 January, the fund stood at £638 18s 8d. The first Spitfire had been flying operationally for months, piloted by various pilots. One contributor was a widow who had saved 480 halfpennies, making a donation of £1.

Russia week began on 8 February with a range of activities and social functions to raise money to help the Russians. To launch the week, George Hicks, Parliamentary Secretary of the Ministry of Works and Buildings, visited the town. By the end of the week £3,095 14s had been raised. Some was used to purchase an X-Ray machine.

Another Warship Week followed in March. Reading's target was £1,200,000. Many businesses bought bonds to show their patriotism, motivate their employees and make money. Suttons bought £1,000 of bonds and gave £25 towards a warship, the same amount the government paid them to store 1,000 tons of coal. The major banks promised £25,000 each. It sounded patriotic but it wasn't their money and it was actually being invested in government bonds so the bank would make the money. This was a little like W. Hinds in Broad Street buying scrap gold because 'Gold means munitions', which meant they bought at below face value and sold it to the government at a higher price to pay America for weapons – profitably patriotic.

Before Warship Week began there were promises of £449,000. To start the week, the Mayor broadcast to the crowd at the Reading v Spurs match, and spoke at the Granby Cinema. Over the weekend £194,498 was raised, by Thursday the total was £719,042. A variety show and auction at the Palace Theatre raised £10,000 for War Bonds, with a bottle of whisky being sold at £1,000 (£46,000 in 2019 prices). The final total, £1,371,962, was well above target. At the same time the town was saving for ten tanks – 'Tanks for Attack' – costing £290,000, raising £308,394.

Local charities also needed money. The Reading Philanthropic Institution assisting local poor asked people to buy their 'Forget-Me-Not' emblems, made by crippled girls. Money raised was disbursed by tickets that could purchase bread, coal, meat, milk and groceries. The Reading Society for the Blind also wanted contributions and held a flag day to raise money.

Instead of money, the RSPCA appealed for leads and dog collars. Although over 500 had been donated at the last appeal, a further 1,000 were needed at rescue centres across the country.

Believing in victory, Burton's were selling a seven guinea model suit for 75 shillings. This was Victory Value and the Victory suit would see the wearer through.

A decision mainly for better-off households was how to replace the iron railings taken for the war effort. Timber was virtually unobtainable, leaving two choices: no fence or a hedge.

Even with rationing there were still plus-size people. Evans Outsize's winter sale offered bargains in sizes which to day equate to 14 plus: WX, OS, XOS and XXOS.

Being overweight is not just a modern phenomenon. Neither is suing for damages. Brian Leonard of Woodcote Road brought an action through his father against Frank Moring, also of Woodcote Road. Moring had seen a parked school bus and pulled out, hitting Leonard. The boy was awarded £500 damages with costs and his father was awarded special damages of £189 3s 9d.

Another parallel with today was a shortage of birds in gardens and the countryside. It was caused by 'the ruthless destruction of nests' the previous spring. People were asked to start feeding the birds again and to leave nests alone. With no fines for stealing eggs it was suggested that unless something was done to halt the decline there would 'be a bad look-out for farmers and fruit growers'.

In 1942 boys born between 1 February 1924 and 31 January 1925 were called up. They were registered and interviewed to encourage them to join youth organisations or to do some form of training or service; when old enough they were called for

Twice Honoured

Mr. H. J. Carswell, of the Merchant Navy, who has been awarded the British Empire Medal and the Distinguished Service Medal. In the last war Mr. Carswell gained the Military Medal.

Mr H.J. Carswell of the Merchant Navy was a very brave man. As a soldier in the Great War he had received the Military Medal and during the Second World War he was awarded the BEM (for bravery), the DSM, and Lloyd's gallantry medal. He survived the war.

military service. Weeks later, boys of 16 and 17 were called to register; shortly after it was the turn of girls aged 16 and 17 to register and women born in 1904.

Initially, the comparative safety of the town had made people lazy about blackout regulations, but by 1942 direct and indirect exposure to the effects of bombing had brought a new understanding between the evacuees and also of the importance of the blackout. As a result, 'the annual number of prosecutions for blackout offences had dropped from nearly 700 to scarcely 250.'

Just as people were getting used to making sure they showed no light, the Luftwaffe lost interest in the town, only visiting once during the year, on 22 June. Again, it was a minor attack on Woodley; just two bombs were dropped, causing no damage. One failed to detonate and was defused.

During the year there was 'a steady drift back of evacuees to their home towns as the intensity of the air raids noticeably decreased.' The 'Closed Town' now had some space. But this was quickly filled when historic towns and cities were bombed during the summer months.

Overall the trend 'was for a movement of evacuees away from Reading, but this to a great extent was counterbalanced by new movements of war-workers into the town'.

Though the chance of a major raid was small, it was still a concern. To help look after babies, three mobile vans were purchased, each fully equipped for child welfare. Known as 'Nannies I, II and III' they were run by three state registered nurses and eight women trained in infant welfare.

In July concerns were expressed over Whitley's air raid shelters. The blame was placed firmly, without any evidence, on mischievous boys; they were blamed for pulling down electric wire and stealing light bulbs and curtains from shelters. Bricks had also been taken from escape holes. With no money to make good the damage, in the event of a raid the shelters would not be as safe or pleasant as when built.

The army's need for more doctors meant both hospitals lost key staff. At the same time they had to identify medical staff who could be transferred to other areas in case of emergency. Also the training of students was curtailed, further decreasing the number of trained staff. Fortunately, local GPs were able to deal with the outpatients. The Royal Berks was again running out of money. By the end of the year it had a deficit of £54,270 with no possibility of further help from the bank; there were threats that it might close at Christmas. However, plans were made to raise further funds from the public during 1943.

The demands of the armed forces affected the staffing of many companies. Women and disabled veterans were two sources for replacements. Phillips & Powis at Woodley became the 'first company in the aircraft industry to test the idea of employing blind people, and employed eight blind men in 1942, including two who had been blinded at Dunkirk and Narvik. After training they soon proved capable of carrying out skilled jobs as efficiently as ordinary employees.' The company was also in the forefront of industrial relations, setting up a Joint Production Board, with equal representation from management and production staff, before it was officially encouraged by the government. There were no strikes or disruptions in the factory during the war.

There were already large numbers of temporary residents in the town, and with the Americans joining the war, there was a further influx. While most were billeted or stationed in the Berkshire countryside, some lived in the town: the South Block of Wilson School was used by the US Army from 1942 until the end of the war. They were not the first foreign troops in the town. By the end of the war members of nearly every Allied nation had been stationed in or around Reading.

Although fruit and vegetables were never rationed, they were not always easy to come by so many households took allotments in response to the government's exhortation to 'Dig for Victory'. Mrs Marsh in Earley, who was looking after four evacuees, ploughed up her garden to grow vegetables. The corporation was prepared, at a price, to deliver sewage sludge as manure to homes and allotments.

This new interest in horticulture resulted in a massive increase in demand for vegetable seeds, so much so that Suttons quickly ran out of runner beans, onions, leeks, cress and, most importantly, of early potatoes.

German involvement in Russia meant that invasion was unlikely, but the possibility was still there. With so many British troops committed in Africa and the Far East, the Home Guard's role increased in importance. At the end of April they prepared for the invasion of Tilehurst on 3 May. An imaginary German force had landed at Weymouth and halted at Andover before attacking in the direction of Reading. It was the job of the Reading Home Guard to man roadblocks to stop the Germans advancing from the west meeting up with those to the east. The exercise also involved residents. They were asked to allow defenders to have easy access to premises, including posting machine guns at windows, accommodate wounded men and give information on any enemy seen, recognisable by their forage caps; the defenders wore steel helmets. Lorries were used as tanks and armoured cars, and attackers and defenders used blank ammunition and an assortment of smoke candles, 'bangs' and other fireworks. Unlike a real invasion, it was scheduled to last for just two hours.

Although women in the Home Guard worked in the anti-aircraft batteries, male chauvinism was never far away. It was proposed to form a local Women's Home Defence Corps, and, given that the Russians were using women in combat roles, including flying fighter planes, this should not have been that difficult an idea to accommodate. Matthew Burns of Blundells Road had other ideas which he expressed publicly. He felt that 'their value would amount to something akin to nil.' This conclusion was obvious: they were physically limited and had a horror of bloodshed, and even if they were courageous it would not carry them through a modern battle. Their forte was not fighting but working in factories and tending the wounded. Mr Burns had missed the point: all they wanted was training in weapons handling in case of need, not to be soldiers. After the inaugural meeting of the organisation in Reading, 75 women enrolled.

Equally prejudiced was the nature of the drive to get more women into the forces. It was essential to keep 'as many men in strictly men's jobs'. Women under 45 who were not involved in essential war work were encouraged to volunteer to join the ATS, WAAF or WRNS as cooks or drivers.

It took nearly three years of war before queueing for a bus became law. From May, the Ministry of War Transport made it compulsory to queue in an orderly manner at recognised bus stops. This coincided with reductions in staffing caused by men being released for the forces, which meant training new people, often women, so the Thames Valley Traction Company asked residents to avoid rush-hour travel and to queue. The number of bus stops was reduced to save fuel and rubber.

Just before Christmas two other changes were implemented to save fuel, oil and rubber: the last petrol bus would leave the town centre at 9 pm every evening, the last trolley

Pilot Officer Thomas Dando, a Wellington bomber pilot in 150 Squadron, was lost on operations at the age of 21 on 11 February 1942.

at 9.30 (9 pm on Sundays). On Sundays there was no service before 1 pm, except buses for war workers.

Another bus-related problem was highlighted by J. Lindsay of Norwood Road, who asked 'those foolish persons who are continually throwing things at pedestrians from the top of the trolley buses, in King's Road and Wokingham Road, to cease doing so. No one knows what damage, or injury, may be done when the missile leaves the hand of the thrower. One lady had a nasty knock on her head in the Wokingham Road and a gentleman had a smart blow on the arm in King's Road.' Patricia Palmer, aged 10, replied that at Alfred Sutton Junior School they were taught how to behave on buses.

In August the Queen visited the town. She spent more than an hour at the Fruit Preserving Centre at McIlroy's store, inspecting the machinery, the supplies of fruit and vegetables, and speaking to the helpers.

Three months later the town was visited by the Deputy Prime Minister who addressed a large gathering at the Odeon Cinema. It was part of a National Rally and in his speech he talked of plans for peace. A few days later the Army Comforts depot in St. Mary's Butts was inspected by the Secretary of State for War, Sir James Grigg.

The King wanted 3 September, the third anniversary of the start of the war, to be a day for prayer and intercession. Ignoring concerns about public assembly and the Luftwaffe, a united service was held in Forbury Gardens at 6.30 pm.

This coincided with yet another appeal for money; this time it was for China.

Later in the year came a rather different appeal: toys. The Mayor wished for unwanted toys to be sent to the Town Hall so they could be given to the wartime nurseries in the town.

Although 3 September was an important anniversary, an advert billed 5 September as Reading's Greatest Day. It was a 'Show…too good to miss!' In Palmer Park there was a military PT display by sixty experts of the Army PT Corps from Aldershot, followed by an athletics match between the AAA and the RAC and district followed by 'a 20 mile road race, Ladies Event, etc'.

The Sunday Armistice commemoration was continued with some churches being full. People were informed that new types of poppy would be sold to conserve materials and that they needed to return them for renovation and resale in 1943. They were also asked to give more generously because the need was much greater. They did: street collections totalled £2,647 18s 8d, £120 more than 1941. Before the final total was in, the Wings for Victory appeal in June was announced – target £1,000,000.

When wages rose the government tried to control inflation by getting people to invest even more in National Savings. The Squanderbug was a very successful campaign to curb spending on non-essentials.

There were Fields of Remembrance at St. Peter's Caversham, and at Christ Church, and again there was no official service at the war memorial. However, the Mayor, along with representatives from other organisations, laid a wreath on the memorial on Armistice Day, and services were held in many local churches where the Two Minutes Silence was observed.

At the same time, the living were given consideration. The Red Cross and St. John's were sending 155,000 parcels a week to PoWs in Europe at a cost of £12,000 a day. Money was needed to maintain this lifeline, so in early December a Prisoners of War Week was held, with another flag day. There was also a gift shop for purchases and donations; one lady gave a diamond necklace anonymously that was sold for 1,000 guineas.

Church bells could not be rung unless there was an invasion. However, across Reading on 15 November they broke their silence summoning people to a thanksgiving service for the victory in North Africa.

Anticipating a cold start to the New Year, the council advised householders to be prepared: make sure the stopcock could be turned off. The council might not be able to assist, plumbers were scarce and replacements might not be available.

With the fourth Christmas of the war, the emphasis was on practicality and patriotism. National Savings was a gift that also provided a Christmas card as part of the purchase. Although non-essential spending was frowned upon there were gifts to buy. The Chamber of Commerce reminded purchasers that shops would be open all day on Wednesday, 23 December – normally a half-day – but would close on Christmas and Boxing Day, reopening on 28 December. For those thinking of going away for the holiday, the message was: stay at home.

Langston & Sons sent out Christmas greetings to their customers and friends and hoped that 1943 would bring them Happiness and Victory. The Co-op wished customers a peaceful Christmas and happier times in the New Year. At the same time as sponsoring an advert for a concert by the Rifle Brigade Band at the Olympia, where a collection for their PoWs would be made, McIlroy's extended season's greetings to customers and friends. *The Standard* wished its readers Christmas greetings and the Mayor and Mayoress of Wokingham extended their warmest greetings to the residents of Wokingham in lieu of sending Christmas cards.

The Standard told readers that 'Love came down at Christmas to bring peace on earth to men of goodwill. Christmas reminds us that we must win the war, but that having won it we have accomplished little unless we win the peace as well.'

The salvage drive continued. The Ministry of Works wanted to know where the council had buried any guns captured in previous wars; they also wanted bandstands. One landmark they took was the covered way from Ascot Racecourse. The Berkshire Mental Hospital offered their obsolete heating system. They also wanted the waterwheels from the Thames tributaries and the tree guards from the town's parks.

Despite rationing, it was reported that Christmas was celebrated in children's homes and hospitals 'in true style', with gifts and parties. The Royal Berks, in festively decked wards, served roast beef, plum pudding and mince pies. On Christmas Eve the nurses sang carols, and on Christmas Day Father Christmas gave every patient a gift. Tea parties were held in every ward on Boxing Day. In the Battle Hospital Christmas dinner consisted of roast pork and poultry, vegetables, plum pudding, ales and mineral waters. Conditions were better than in Nazi-occupied Europe where Greece needed 10,000 tons more wheat than were available and in Belgium where there was a trebling of premature births and high death rate of infants caused by food shortages.

Football continued throughout the war but the only continuity was the name of the team. With many players conscripted, guest players filled gaps and although the standard of the game was not as high, thousands went weekly to watch their team. The Boxing Day match at Elm Park, when Reading lost 4-3 to Aldershot, included three players who happened to be in the area: Pescod (Halifax), Clayton (Notts County) and Laird (St. Mirren). The collection during the match raised £28 13s 9d for the PoW Fund. The previous day at Aldershot, Reading had held the home team to a draw.

Being taken PoW generally meant surviving the war. Driver Jack Naish, Royal Berkshire Regiment, was one of many who did not survive captivity. He died in a PoW camp in Poland on 31 December 1942, leaving a wife and four sons.

Christmas 1942 was a stay-at-home Christmas – a period of sober rejoicing at the family hearth, but without the special niceties of pre-war days. In his Christmas broadcast, the King told his people that the tasks before them may be even harder than those they had performed already, but they must be accomplished to reach the final goal – victory and peace.

Once again at Christmas the wish was happiness and, of course, Victory.

CHAPTER FIVE

1943

Ring out the Old – Ring in the New! How did Reading feel about it? *The Standard* probably summed it up for most people in the town: 'Today is New Year's Day. We have said good-bye to 1942. Let us not think unkindly of it. During its course we have endured trials and suffered reverses, but we have also achieved successes. And it is because of those very successes that we face the year ahead hopefully and confidently. We believe we are on the right road to victory. We must keep to that road and to do so we must take care that there will be no relaxation of effort in any department of national industry.' Karandash wrote: 'The now dead year has held within its course events that will never fade from the history of our race.'

As for resolutions, the government wanted everyone to resolve to cut down on all forms of fuel, to salvage regularly and save as much as possible; it also wanted everyone to 'Dig for Victory' to grow more potatoes and reduce the shipping space taken up by wheat. 'To waste bread is to help the U-boats in their deadly task.' The Ministry of Food suggested that cooked and dried potato could be used in place of flour. It also wanted households to eat potatoes for breakfast three times a week and make them the main meal once a week. Instead of eating second helpings of other food, a potato should be eaten instead and they asked the housewife to 'serve potatoes in other ways than "plain boiled"'. Reading council emphasised the importance of the task by asking everyone to dig up their lawn and grow crops;

if they couldn't, the council would put them in contact with someone who would, to the mutual benefit of both parties.

The Thames Valley Traction Company asked people to not flag down buses between stops as this added wear to the tyres which were in very short supply.

Milk bottles were also in short supply. From 21 February, the Co-op advised that the misuse or destruction of milk bottles or keeping them too long was an offence. A quick return would aid the national effort. From the end of February, milk, like bread, was to be delivered without rounds overlapping to save fuel.

Using less water saved fuel. It was an offence to use it for anything other than domestic purposes, as Dr Cane of Tilehurst Road found out. His house had been kept under observation by Inspector Williams of the Water Undertaking. He was reported for using water to fill his ornamental pond. His concern was the wellbeing of his goldfish, but was told that they were a luxury and was fined £1 with 10s costs.

After complaints about the number of bus tickets not being recycled, Reading was involved in a nationwide book salvage drive. In two weeks in March they hoped to collect 250,000 to turn into new paper. The previous collection raised issues about valuable items being shredded, so the government set up panels to inspect every book collected and identify those worth keeping. The target was reached, with 8.5 per cent going to the forces, 2.4 per cent to bombed-out libraries, the rest were pulped.

There was also a collection of kitchen scraps to feed chicken and pigs, and a campaign to get everyone doing a full spring clean that would produce salvageable material. The Mayor also wanted blood. Reading held an Army Blood Transfusion week, wanting 10,000 people to give blood. To motivate people, a ceremonial march processed from the Cattle Market around the town to Abbot's Walk Gate.

Reading had been more sober in 1942 than in the previous year. Only eleven locals had been prosecuted for drunkenness, the remainder had been temporary residents. In 1941 proceedings had been taken against 73 males and 11 females, in 1942 the numbers were 41 and 4. The most impressive case of drunkenness was Richard Dyke, a civil servant. Pleading not guilty, after hearing the police evidence he pleaded guilty. On 3 May he had been arrested for being helplessly drunk, fined 10s and released, he was later brought in and charged with the same offence. It was also noted that insobriety increased with age.

Drink related offences were common: there were four incidents reported in the 6 August edition of *The Standard* alone. Two drunken soldiers stole meat pies, Rose Collins was incapable of standing and had to be taken in an ambulance to the police station, a Canadian soldier pleaded guilty to being drunk and disorderly on Blagrave Street, and Winifred Bartlett pleaded guilty to being drunk: she could not stand without assistance.

The courts were always busy. Reginald Hall of Blenheim Road, Caversham, was charged with bigamy. A week later at the Berkshire Assizes there were seven bigamy cases; while drunkenness decreased, bigamy increased. A 15-year-old boy was charged with stealing a white rabbit; Lavinia Bungay was placed on probation for behaviour liable to cause a breach of the peace. Her crime: defending the honour of Reading women. Eldridge Taylor was remanded in custody for wearing the uniform of a Merchant Navy officer, and two caravan dwellers were fined £5 for keeping their caravan for more than forty-two days on the same piece of ground. George Lucas was bound over for two years and fined 34s costs for entering No. 7, Victoria Square, for no lawful purpose and by his conduct disturbing the peace of residents in a manner calculated to provoke a breach of the peace. In June, what must have been a record was the case of Sidney Fuller (alias Newton), a 72-year-old who was jailed for a month. His crime was travelling without a ticket; he had been convicted over 100 times previously for similar offences.

There was no trial for the unknown female child whose body was found in the main porch of St. Mary's Church under a sandbag. The coroner's verdict was 'murder by some person or persons unknown'. The post-mortem examiner said that 'the body was contained in a brown paper carrier bag' and was 'wrapped in a child's blue woollen dress, a woman's powder-blue knitted sleeveless cardigan and a mixture blue lock-knit slip. A handkerchief with the initial "G" in a corner had been placed in the mouth, and a tape was tied round the neck. Death was due to suffocation from the handkerchief and strangulation by the tape.'

In the same edition was the case of Ellen Sawyer summoned for wilfully neglecting her nine children; she was not jailed but Emily Webb received a three months' custodial sentence for neglecting her two children. Two families were fined for not sending their children to school. Mrs Schultz of Romsey Road had not sent her son to school on 139 occasions and her daughter 135 times, out of a maximum 145 sessions. This was due to illness and a lack of shoes. Henry Biddel of South Street had also kept his five children from school; three of them had not attended at all. This he claimed was because of illness: quinsy, diphtheria and measles. Both were fined £5; in Biddel's case if he failed to send them to school he was to be imprisoned for a month.

The Chief Constable for Berkshire's annual report showed during 1942 there had been 100 cases of burglary/housebreaking, an increase of three on 1941; the value of property stolen was £10,306 of which just £94 had been recovered. Shop-breaking and other breaking offences had increased by 33 to 130. There were 2,054 cases of larceny and 267 indictable offences. Non-indictable offences showed a decrease of 1,708. He also reported that deaths caused by motor vehicles in the county had increased in 1942, with 113 killed (including five children), 18 more than in 1941, but the number of injured had fallen by 337 to 1,511.

It was reported that, nationally, children aged 3 to 7 were the most vulnerable, that most accidents occurred between 3 and 6 pm, and that Sunday was the safest day. Proving the point, the 28 May edition reported the death of Ann Andrews, aged 5. She had been hit by her father's lorry; the time of the accident was not recorded. Nationally, the number of child fatalities fell from 108 to 89. Figures released later in the year showed that 30,000 people had been killed and upwards of 500,000 injured on the road in the first three and a half years of the war.

Other deaths included Charles Smith, who died of pneumonia after suffering multiple injuries when he fell off a trolley bus; Martin Zetland, aged 10, drowned in the Thames; Stephen Calvert, a member of the Home Guard, drowned in the Kennet; Frederick Grigg was killed when a tree fell on him as he was chopping it down; 3-year-old Betty Richardson died of shock caused by burning: she had set fire to her bedclothes in her bedroom; Frank Holloway of Luckmore Drive gassed himself while his wife was out. In Henley, a female shop assistant was shot dead in Greys Road and an American soldier was taken to hospital with a bullet wound to the mouth.

Each edition of *The Standard* carried a roll of honour; the 1 January edition was no exception, but it was shorter than those in recent weeks with just two names. Sergeant Foale of Winchester Road was safe in an Italian PoW Camp. Just two weeks later, notification of the death of Sapper Stevenson in an Italian PoW camp must have given some pause for thought. Later in the war many PoWs in Italian hands escaped, some turning up months later. One such escapee was Craftsman/Private Lickfield of 32 Drayton Road who had been in hiding for ten months when he was found.

News was received that any letter sent to a PoW in Japanese hands had to be typewritten; fortunately hundreds of volunteer professional typists were prepared to help. In an attempt to console families, Mr King, Controller of the Far East Section of the PoW Department of the Red Cross and St. John, deliberately lied, telling those present at the Reading Town Hall meeting that rumours of bad treatment were untrue: there had been no atrocities and that apart from shortages of medical supplies and a different diet, everything was fine.

Sister E. English SRN/TANS, eldest daughter of Mr and Mrs English of Green Road, was reported missing at sea. She was coming home after serving eighteen months in Nigeria. Amazingly, she had been torpedoed on the way out to West Africa as well.

Later in the year, Section Officer Judy Chandler of the WAAF died. She was just 21.

After reading about such losses, many would have had little sympathy with conscientious objectors. Probably some would have thought the judge lenient when he sentenced Gilbert Duck, a Jehovah's Witness, to three months' imprisonment for refusing to a range of non-combatant duties for over three years.

On 13 January, the National Service Act was extended to men aged 46 and women aged 31. Men were to join the armed forces but women could opt for industrial war work, become a nurse or join the forces.

For those in employment, absenteeism was punishable by a fine. Typical examples were Annie Klein, who missed three non-continuous days and was fined £3 with 12s costs; Gladys Hill was fined 30s for each of three non-continuous days absence

SISTER E. ENGLISH

Sister Eileen English of the Territorial Nursing Service, was coming home after 18 months nursing in Nigeria when the ship was torpedoed. She is commemorated in Brookwood cemetery.

because she had been absent 25 times and late on 11 occasions; and Elsie Green who had previously appeared before the court for absenteeism was fined £6 for the three summonses or fourteen days' imprisonment.

Stories of bravery and amazing feats must have been welcome after reading the casualty lists. One story involved 21-year-old Squadron Leader Isted of Caversham. He was awarded the DFC after a 17-hour patrol over the Atlantic with another plane during which they attacked eleven U-boats and probably sank two. At the same time, Squadron Leader Davies of Eldon Square was awarded a bar to his AFC; he already had the DFC. Possibly the most impressive awards were to H. Carswell of the Merchant Navy. So far in the war he had been awarded the British Empire Medal and the Distinguished Service Medal. They were not his first awards: in the Great War as a soldier he had been awarded the Military Medal. Reading pilot Flight Lieutenant Fraser made the news when he and a pilot from Bracknell flew the King to North Africa after the defeat of the Axis forces.

Good news came from the Ministry of Food: it announced that registered consumers would receive one egg a week but couldn't guarantee delivery because of transportation difficulties. When available, retailers would put a notice in their shop window.

Reading was international news during January. Recorded stories about life in the town were broadcast to men serving in the Middle East. The items included reminiscences from PC Hayes who had spent the previous sixteen years in a box at Cemetery Junction directing traffic, news about Reading FC, greetings from a Reading University student, how well the People's Pantry was doing, the effect of the war on Sutton's seeds experimental ground, and greetings from Simonds Brewery.

Reading was also on the BBC, after the nine o'clock news, with 'the thrilling story of a Reading woman's experiences in Burma at the time of the Japanese invasion'. Miss Rosina Simmonds was nursing in Mandalay but managed to escape to India.

The international aspect of Reading was reinforced in July. On Independence Day, St. Laurence's Hall was officially opened as an American club for visitors from the United States.

Even with all the restrictions people still had fun. In just one week *The Standard* recorded three large gatherings and the formation of a monthly nursery workers' club. The Reading Christian Spiritualist Church entertained 60-70 children from some of the poorest families in the town with every child leaving with fruit, and a bag of sweets even though they were rationed. Miss Marie Hyde, the well-known leader of the popular Accordion Dance Band, celebrated her coming of age and engagement with 100 guests, while at their institute in Pell Street, about 100 guests attended the annual party for the deaf and dumb. Naturally part of the entertainment was a silent film.

Throughout the year the number of evacuees fell constantly, but as in the previous year the fall was more than countered by an increase in those employed in the war industries. The population of the town again expanded.

Reading continued to have Royal visitors. In March, the Duchess of Kent inspected Civil Defence workers and visited Holybrook House day nursery.

The only air raid to have any major impact on the town was one of a number of minor incidents during February. In the preceding days, the Luftwaffe had bombed areas mostly across the south-east of England. Apart from London and Sunderland, the targets were small towns such as Worthing where eight people were killed, and Eastbourne with fourteen fatalities. Fortunately, by this stage of the war, while still deadly, the Luftwaffe was no longer capable of the mass raids of previous years. Much of the bombing was done by fighter-bombers, often looking for targets of opportunity rather than bombing war industry. Consequently damage was rarely substantial. Although the raid of 10 February is the most significant, it is interesting to note that the greatest number of bombs was dropped on the town during 1940-41: around 400 incendiaries and over 100 high explosive bombs.

The raids on 10 February were more dangerous. During scattered bombing across Berkshire, Hampshire and Sussex, 77 people were killed, and 123 seriously injured. Reading fared the worst with 41 killed, while 19 died in the bombing of Newbury. At around 16.35 hrs, machine gun fire was heard, followed by four explosions. The first bomb hit Simonds Brewery and passed through a shed before detonating. It caused a small fire but no casualties. The second passed through the Reading Trades Union Club, bounced off a wall, crossed Minster Street and hit Wellsteeds department store about twenty-five feet above the pavement. The explosion demolished the rear of the building and partially demolished the front; surrounding buildings were also damaged. Blast and flying debris damaged buildings on the south side of Broad Street. Two children and a man were killed, Betty Parsons, Violet Brown and James Doran. A further nine were injured with others being treated at the Simonds Brewery first aid post. As it was early closing day, there were few people about so the total casualty list was considerably smaller than if it had been earlier in the day.

Seconds later the third bomb fell on the 'People's Pantry' where many had left their seats to get a view of what was happening. As they moved to the door the bomb exploded causing the roof to collapse and bury customers and staff. Like the second bomb, it had a time delay fuse, allowing it to hit the wooden rear extension to a shop and pass through the top storey of the building next door before clipping the corner of the first floor of the restaurant. 'The explosion damaged a 64 foot long run of wall in the Arcade next to the Pantry, and brought down two bays of the restaurant's roof, causing a third to "hinge" into the kitchen… In effect this dropped the restaurant into its own basement, and dropped its roof on top of it.'

'The majority of those killed or injured were victims of *Falling debris and…flying missiles such as the bricks of the wall near the bomb.* Ten bodies were found in the yard outside the restaurant, with *Four headless corpses in the restaurant in line with the detonation of the bomb.* One victim was blown into the corner of a shop in the arcade, *another into the Transfer station at the back of Odd Fellows Hall.*' In the basement nine staff were injured and in the kitchen a further five suffered injuries with one losing her right arm. Two workers were killed in the arcade, as was a Post Office worker, and two in the restaurant. Edith Osbourne and Emily Parker had gone in for a cup of tea. Their bodies were identified the next day. Three people were killed in Market Place and Market Street and four at 29 Market Place. Fortunately for those attending a WVS course at the headquarters in Market Passage they had vacated the building five minutes before it was demolished.

A fourth bomb, released almost immediately, landed near St. Laurence's church. It passed through the upper floor of the People's Pantry demolishing the BBC transmitter in the attic, injuring two. The frontage of Blandy's solicitors collapsed into the crater and the blast caused damage to the church. The blast also brought down the ceiling of the Mayor's Parlour, blew in windows and killed a woman in a basement passage.

Reading's only major raid was a simple target of convenience; a hit and run with no real purpose other than to kill and damage. This shows the devastation after a bomb landed on the People's Pantry on 10 February 1943.

A street-view showing the damage to the church and surrounding buildings caused by the second bomb.

Only yards away from the bombing Marjorie Culham was attending a meeting at the main post office in Friar Street. She recalled the event clearly: 'Just after 4.30pm when the meeting finished, the sirens sounded. The noise of the bombs dropping and anti-aircraft fire was incredible and we stayed in the basement until the ALL CLEAR. We emerged to a scene of absolute devastation, Friar Street was covered in broken glass and the council brought out snow ploughs to clear it so that the buses could run.'

Whether it was before, during, or after the bombing, what is certain is that parts of the town were machine-gunned. 'The bullets struck in an area from Market Place out to a cold storage depot at the foot of Norcot Road in Tilehurst and up into Hemdean, Albert and Blenheim Roads in Caversham.' The only known injury caused by bullets is Mrs Meadowcraft who was hit at 149 Hemdean Road. The council school in Hemdean recorded in its log that bullets had damaged walls, ceilings, windows and roofs but no one was hurt.

'Of the 86 casualties taken to Reading Hospital, one was found dead on arrival, 42 were admitted to the emergency Benyon Ward and the remainder were treated in the casualty department.' One of those injured that day was the future creator of Paddington Bear, Michael Bond. Three surgeons worked continuously for three-and-a-half hours treating the seriously wounded: thirty-one people required operations, including two amputations. The hospital ran out of blood: 300 pints were used in a matter of hours, necessitating the recall of donors the next day to replenish stocks. Meanwhile, the search for survivors and the dead went on into the next day.

One lucky survivor of the attack was Derek Chamberlain, then aged 14. Walking outside the arcade, he saw a bomb falling just yards away. It exploded as he began to run and he was blown twenty yards through the arcade. Apart from ringing ears and the sound of falling glass and masonry he could not recall much until he awoke in hospital. His injuries were extensive: 'a fractured skull, broken right femur, broken arm and shrapnel in his back.' He spent the next eight months in hospital.

An early hour was selected for the funerals of some of those killed to reduce the number of sightseers. 'The bodies were enclosed in coffins of unpolished elm and the graves were draped in purple, floral tributes being placed at the head of each. One grave contained two unidentified bodies and another, the separate coffins of two little children. A large floral cross composed of carnations, daffodils and arum lilies and inscribed "From the Corporation, to express the sympathy of the towns-people" was placed on end in the centre.' There was another cross from the WVS. An air raid distress fund set up by the Mayor raised over £157 in just over a week.

Private Miles saw the attack as a chance to make some money. He was charged with stealing from premises which had been vacated by reason of enemy attack.

The total death toll is still uncertain. One report gives 41 killed but there were only 37 named deaths and two unknowns; of these 39, three died later of their injuries. Most of the deaths occurred in the People's Pantry. Across the country that day another 40 people were killed by enemy action, 15 of them in Newbury.

It was not immediately apparent to those who lived away from the town centre, unless they knew someone involved, that there had been an incident. With strict censorship of sensitive information that could aid the enemy, the raid was acknowledged in the press but its location was not given.

To the nation it was simply a Home Counties town; even the Reading papers could not mention the name although everyone knew where it was. It was not even a lead story, appearing with reports on education in Berkshire, the findings of an inquest on a 19-year-old who died after having two teeth removed, a 40-year-old woman who drowned in the Kennet as a result of the blackout, the story of a fracas in the Cross Keys public house, the curious case of the drunk on the railway line, and notes on the annual meeting of the local Free Church Federal Council. It was not until the end of April that Reading was named as the bombed town.

As well as giving for the war effort, residents were also asked to dig deep into their pockets to assist The Royal Berks. Fundraising was so successful that by the end of August all their debt had been repaid. The Debt Reduction Appeal Committee was then renamed the Hospital Appeal Committee; its purpose to increase the hospital's income.

The People's Pantry had been destroyed and not rebuilt, being replaced after the war by the Bristol and West Arcade. In April 1944 a new People's Pantry opened at 23 Cross Street.

In April, Robert Capa, the well-known war photographer, was commissioned to photograph the Woodley aircraft factory at work. He was followed by Feliks Topolski, a Polish artist, who had been 'commissioned to depict working scenes in the factory and a set of eight coloured pencil sketches was subsequently published in *Milestones Nineteen Hundred & Forty Six*'.

While most people were concerned about just surviving the war, some politicians were looking ahead to peace. Something

Reading's Education Board had to come to terms with was the government White Paper on post-war education. In the post-war era, every child over 11 would be provided with secondary education till the age of 15. One question was where to build the schools?

Another problem was the baby boom. The birth rate had steadily increased between 1933 and 1938 and although it had fallen slightly on the outbreak of war, by the end of 1943 it had passed the 1938 level. 'Reading's rising birth rate meant that the Maternity Department was becoming a significant part of Battle's growing work load.' Caversham Grove Maternity Home in Emmer Green had been established to deal with evacuees, but they were only part of the boom. In the first six months they turned away sixty-five Reading women who then delivered their baby in Battle.

Not all the babies were wanted. In May a baby was found abandoned in a telephone kiosk at the junction of Vastern and Caversham Road. He was about four months old and, apart from having been abandoned, had been well cared for. There were no clues to aid in identifying the parents.

The housing problem surfaced again, especially in Whitley. Overcrowding had been highlighted before the war and conditions during the conflict made things worse – 'following an eruption of damage to property and of homes on the estate in 1943.' Dr Berry, a local GP, Labour Councillor George Stent and the Reverend Woods, Vicar Of Christ Church, compiled a survey of conditions on the estate. The subjective data divided the households into four classes:

- 20 per cent – houses unclean to a major degree. The atmosphere of filth and squalor is striking, and there is gross overcrowding
- 20 per cent – have many of the above faults, but to a considerably lesser degree. Some families had income in excess of £500 a year
- 40 per cent – homes are reasonably well cared for with little or no overcrowding
- 20 per cent – really good homes that were admirable in every way.

The report suggested measures to improve the area: 'A public telephone kiosk, public conveniences, improved public transport, better provision for shopping, more chemist or dispensary facilities, more places for meetings and social functions, an indoor swimming pool, outdoor sporting facilities such as a tennis court and bowling green, and the planting of more trees.' It was suggested more midwives were needed on the estate but the wife of the priest in charge of St. Agnes argued for more birth control facilities.

Back in 1939 concerns had been expressed about the effect of the war on children's behaviour. In March *The Chronicle* reported on the prosecution of a woman in Dawlish Road by the NSPCC who had wilfully neglected her stepchildren – their birthmother had been killed in an air raid on London; 'they were found locked in a bedroom, malnourished, riddled with vermin and covered in sores.' Later in the month a mother of nine, living in Callington Road, was found guilty of neglecting the diet and health of her children by leaving them at home for long periods while she worked. Her life was not easy; she was the victim of domestic violence by her husband. Three months later Doris Grubb was imprisoned for two months for neglecting her son.

The survey was completed for positive reasons but nationally it was bad press for Reading. Prospective Parliamentary Labour candidate Ian Mikardo took the findings to a national paper, the *News Chronicle,* which highlighted the problems of overcrowding: 'Thirteen decent people have to sleep in three tiny rooms.'

Whitley was never targeted by the Luftwaffe – fortunately, because many of its air raid shelters were unusable. The *News Chronicle* article revealed Whitley's 'foulest features – the street air raid shelters. Some have doors, most appear to be unlocked or completely open. Almost all are used for refuse sweepings. Some are used as lavatories (the only 'public' lavatory on the estate was put up by the bus company for its own drivers and conductors). A number are so unbearably foul that they cannot be described. And among them, the children of Whitley play.' Needless to say, such comment did not go unnoticed locally.

Some residents felt that great harm had been done to the estate, but at the same meeting, one woman retorted that they didn't have 17 people living in their house. There was also resentment about the evacuees and people billeted on them. What was agreed was that many of the homes were in need of repair and painting. Eventually a few were painted.

Caversham Park had been requisitioned at the start of the war to become a hospital. Instead it was purchased by BBC as a monitoring station. Many of those who manned the listening stations were refugees who had to listen to often tragic news from their homelands.

Ceremonial parades, often with weapons and drill demonstrations, marked the third anniversary of the Home Guard. In Woodley they joined in with the Wings for Victory parade. The largest parade was held by the 7th (Reading) Battalion which also included a weapons display to a large crowd.

In June there was Wings for Victory week: target £1,000,000; enough to buy twenty-five Lancaster bombers. Between 15 and 22 May, a wide range of demonstrations and activities were organised in Sonning. 'The events included a Flying Demonstration and Exhibition on the Recreation Ground, 'tank-ambush' by the local Home Guard, a Whist-Drive, an Open Air Dance and Horse Show in Holme Park.' It was hoped that the recent victory in North Africa would stimulate giving and lending. In Reading there was a Heinkel He III in the Odeon carpark; looking was free, to walk through the plane cost 1d.

Naturally schools were keenly involved in such fund-raising activities with Christ Church School raising £72, £30 over its target, and Earley St. Peter's showing the relative affluence of the area, raising £150. In five days £642,050 was raised. A week later the total was £1,390,106. In recognition of the success of the savings drive, Reading was awarded a plastic plaque. Days later, in Heelas' store the RAF displayed a number of photographs to show the work being done by Bomber Command.

Companies willingly invested money in War Bonds which paid 2½ per cent interest; an attractive proposition to patriots and those with spare cash. Sutton's Seeds again took the lead and

Another major fund raiser was the Wings for Victory Week. The plan was to purchase twenty-five Lancaster bombers, but the money collected allowed them to purchase an extra ten. The advert was paid for by Milward & Sons.

invested £10,000, and most major banks later invested £25,000. For people investing their money in National War Bonds or Savings Bonds they would receive no return until the early 1950s and until sometime in the 1960s respectively.

The next recycling drive was for metal: the Berkshire Scrap Metal Recovery Drive. The 450,000 tons of iron railings from three million homes was insufficient. Mobile teams would call on farmers to find and remove old machinery, and households could give or sell the Ministry scrap by the ton. 'Scrap metal is not a romantic job,' a collector explained, 'it is just hard slogging all the way.' People who hid their railings for use after the war could be fined and have them requisitioned.

Old rags were the next commodity needed to help prosecute the war successfully. They were wanted by the RAF to make felt to insulate high-flying planes.

Again people were urged to holiday at home to free space for essential travel. The programme of events was launched to coincide with 'Wings for Victory'. One highlight was a Carnival in King's Meadow on the August Bank Holiday, followed by a Gala Ball and Cabaret in the Town Hall. For those just wanting a day out, Salters were still running services up and down the Thames.

AWARDED THE D.F.M.

Flight Sergeant Sydney G. Keatley, R.A.F.V.R., now Pilot Officer, son of Mr. and Mrs. Keatley, of 49, Norfolk

FLT.-SGT. S. G. KEATLEY

Road, Reading, who, as announced last week, has been awarded the D.F.M.

Air Gunner Flight Sergeant Keatley of 49 Norfolk Road was in the papers for being awarded the DFM.

The fourth anniversary of the war was a National Day of Thanksgiving, Prayer and Dedication. Some children were allowed to listen to the special radio broadcast instead of doing their lessons and a united service was held in Forbury Gardens in the early evening.

Jumping the gun again, the Allotment Association held its 3rd Annual Victory Gardening Show. It was raising funds for the Red Cross and St. John Fund. There were over eighty competitive classes with free entry – rabbit entries cost – and nearly £100 in prizes. Sonning had held a Victory Garden Produce Show two weeks earlier.

Reading Stadium held a very successful horse show in September with the 379 entries being classed as pre-war standard. It was another way of getting money: this time for Russia's wounded horses through the Animals (Allies) Fund.

The Berkshire Assizes heard an unusual case in October. Nine Canadian soldiers were committed for trial charged with robbery with violence from American soldiers in Reading. The case was postponed with just two plaintiffs being detained. Eventually one was convicted and sentenced to eighteen months and birched, the other received six months. Shortly after, two other Canadians were convicted of robbery with violence and sentenced to twelve months imprisonment and twelve strokes of the birch.

For those with time on their hands after a hard days' work there were plenty of options to help the war effort. For the dark evenings *The Standard* suggested Home Guarding, Fire Guarding, Civil Defence or work in a munitions plant. Alternatively, the Reading Cage Bird Society was busy arranging their annual show, or the Central Ballroom in Friar Street was offering practice dances with tuition twice a week, and the cinemas offered a wide range of films. For those who preferred sport, Reading FC was still playing regular fixtures, and there was pigeon racing. Offering a more active participation were cycling clubs like the Bon Amis, and for people who enjoyed smoky atmospheres there was the local billiards league.

There were a number of happy family reunions in October when a group of PoWs was repatriated from Germany: Major L. Griffith of St. Peter's Avenue, Sapper Sidney Catt of Queen's Road, Private Arthur Gowers of Gratwicke Road and Private Golder of Vachel Road. Another surprise arrival was Able Seaman Breadmore of Thirlmere Avenue. He was home on leave after escaping from his PoW camp in Italy.

Armistice Day was again marked quietly. However, this did not stop the Earley and East Reading British Legion having a parade. They marched from Palmer Park to Earley St. Peter's Church and after a service and wreath-laying proceeded to Reading Cemetery to lay another wreath. The money collected was £3,274 4s 6d, £500 more than 1942.

Before the poppy appeal money was counted, the collectors were out again. This time it was for the YMCA; they wanted £4,000.

For the fifth Christmas of the war customers were informed that shops would close on Friday evening, 24 December, and reopen on 29 December. There was the usual reduction in public transport.

There was less to buy as many articles were rationed, and the government asked people not to be Squanderbugs but use their money to buy War Savings Gift Tokens. Everyone was asked to save coal: 5lbs saved would produce 100 bullets for a Bren gun. Readers were asked, 'How many bullets a day will you produce?' To supplement coal stocks, Toomers in Friar Street had plentiful supplies of logs.

Over Christmas there were plenty of films to see: the Palace Theatre was offering *1066 And All That*, with the yearly pantomime – *Aladdin & His Wonderful Lamp* – starting on Boxing Day. There was a Christmas Eve and Boxing Night Dance in the Town Hall, while the Olympia had dances on Boxing Night and New Year's Eve.

The Chief Constable's final report for the year recorded an increase in burglary/housebreaking. There had been less minor crime but more of it was committed by minors. 'During the quarter, 12 persons were killed and 25 injured on the road: an increase of two deaths but a decrease of 51 injured. Two children of school age were killed, 30 were injured.'

At the Berkshire Epiphany Quarter Sessions, the judge sentenced probably the most stupid burglar to eight months hard labour. Instead of escaping with the stolen goods, he sat down and started drinking the gin he had found. He was still sitting drinking when the police arrived. His partner had run away.

Reading Wing, Air Training Corps, wished all ex-cadets serving in the forces 'Hearty Greetings and Best Wishes for 1944', and invited boys aged 15¼-17¾ years to join to train for the RAF, Fleet Air Arm or as an Army Glider Pilot. 'Stand to your Horses. Best Wishes for Christmas and 1944,' were the greetings from the 1st/1st Berkshire RHA. Dunsters of Reading

BASIL FRANK TAYLOR   WILLIAM JOHN BALDWIN

Two good friends who died just a day apart. Sergeant William Baldwin, 218 Squadron, of 23 Newark Street, lost his life on operations on 22 November, aged 21. Sergeant Basil Taylor was killed in an accident the next day. He is buried in Reading cemetery.

told readers that good times always come again. They wished their customers good luck and admitted that it was 'no good wishing you a Merry Christmas' but that everyone could look forward to the New Year in confidence with perhaps the next Christmas one when the 'lights could go up and the boys were home again'.

The Standard told readers to make the best and most of it, asking that every scrap of Christmas waste went to salvage. Twelve letters made a box for rifle cartridges, an average Christmas card made fifty wads for cartridges, a breakfast cereal box made a demolition carton and several cartridge cup plugs. Where they got the idea that paper was used to make propellers from is unclear and how the high grade paper on board HMS *Duke of York* helped sink the *Scharnhorst* was not explained.

It was a traditional Christmas for most. Parcels of toys came from America and US soldiers gave their sweet ration 'to the children they entertained. There were parties for evacuees and orphans, and at the children's homes in the town a happy time was spent, the festivities lasting several days. The sick were not forgotten and in all hospitals and homes special events were arranged, and Father Christmas paid his annual visit distributing gifts to patients.'

Reading Post Office recorded that 1,473,027 letters were posted in just twelve days before Christmas, with 224,669 items on the last day for guaranteed delivery. On 24 December, 27,000 telegrams were sent, mostly greetings. Considerable time was

Reading had its quota of oranges, and this picture shows a queue in the Market on Saturday.

Non-essential imported foodstuffs arrived irregularly, and when they did, queues were quick to form. This is the market on Saturday; the food was a consignment of oranges.

wasted on rewrapping parcels, working out almost indecipherable addresses and dealing with parcels that broke or were too wet. The sorting office contained a multitude of foodstuffs: pieces of beef, poultry, pastry, apples – even lemons and oranges. Fruit was a particular problem: it ripened in transit, saturated the wrappings, got ruined in transit and wet the other parcels, often making the ink run.

On 31 December Tutty's of London Street wished their customers New Year Greetings. At the same time as wishing citizens a good New Year, the Mayor also asked them to dip into their pockets to support the India Famine Relief Fund. The papers warned residents not to throw paper in the streets as it was an offence. Readers were warned of another waste paper drive starting on 10 January. More of the same should have been the message.

One person enjoyed the New Year's Eve celebration but to her cost. Gwendoline Battersby of Newcastle Road was fined £3 for being absent from her shift on 31 December, being not in a fit condition to work. She was fined a further £6 for absenteeism.

CHAPTER SIX

1944

In January 1917, the Reading papers made no comment about the coming year but the vicar of Earley St. Peter's expressed his thoughts to his parishioners: 'A New Year is just opening upon us. It may well be one of the most important years in our nation's history; may God bring us safely through it.' Writing in January, the vicar of Sonning also felt that the coming year would be important: 'We can look forward to the New Year with every confidence that it will bring peace to Europe, and freedom and food to the populations lying under the cruel rule of the German aggressor.'

The Standard started the year with the usual Roll of Honour. There were seven photos of a patriotic Tilehurst family. Mrs Stacey of Norcot Road had five sons in the forces. Beating the Staceys were the Sherwoods of Great Knollys Street, with six sons in the forces.

These were followed by a piece on the receipt of a card from a soldier who had been missing for two years and a report on the death of a PoW in Japanese hands.

In the same issue the Joint War Organisation of the Red Cross and St. John asked for help. They had a charity (gift) shop in Blagrave Street where donated articles were sold to raise funds for Berkshire PoWs.

Some stories were good for civilian morale and also showed that Reading men were doing their bit. Flight Lieutenant Hall, an old Leighton Park schoolboy had played his part: at the end of January he shot down two German bombers in one night.

Lieutenant Commander Abram had his exploits compared with Trafalgar. Commanding the sloop HMS *Magpie* on patrol with four other sloops, he sank six U-boats, three of them in sixteen hours. Their reception on return was recorded the *Daily Telegraph*, 'the greatest given by the Navy to the Navy since the war began'. The ship was later adopted by the Rotary Club of Reading. Whether this story is true is open to some doubt, but the boat was certainly involved in three U-boat sinkings on two separate occasions.

The local record for the most wounds sustained on active service went to Private William Simmonds of Highgrove Street. By February he had been wounded five times and suffered from malaria. Another record holder was Horace Carswell. A year earlier he had been decorated for bravery at sea: it was his third bravery award in two world wars. This time it was the Lloyd's War Medal for bravery at sea on the freighter *Empire Tide* bound for Russia. In late September three Reading railway workers, Harold Dowle, Arthur Griffin and William Ward, received the British Empire Medal for brave conduct. A tank wagon train collided with a stationary freight train, derailing eight wagons; the leading four caught fire, and the open wagon next to the train was crushed and burnt out. Although the petrol was alight they managed to uncouple the train and remove it before it was destroyed.

The call-up age was 18 but anyone could serve in the NAAFI. They were advertising for youths aged between 16 and 17½ to assist in naval canteens. Unable to fight, they could serve on a fighting ship as a civilian where they could be killed. To serve in a war zone they had to be 17 and have parental consent.

Among the petty crimes and bigamy cases was an attempted murder: 'Drove lorry at wife' was the headline. The accused was charged with three counts of causing grievous bodily harm to his wife with intent, maliciously driving a motor lorry at her and causing her harm while having charge of a lorry. Just before the incident she claimed her husband had said to her: 'I will finish you off.' Pleading innocence he told the court he did not know his wife had been hit by his lorry. He was found guilty of causing bodily harm by wilful misconduct.

Summing up, the judge stated that he had deliberately knocked down his wife in a fit of ill-temper and that he was fortunate she had not been more seriously injured; that and his good character meant that he would be sentenced for only four months.

Absenteeism and lateness for work impacted the war effort and were punishable in law. Not turning up for your fire-watch shift could result in unnecessary casualties. Edward Cleere of Highgrove Terrace pleaded guilty to seven summonses for failing to perform fireguard duties between November and the end of December. He was fined 3s for each summons even though he had twelve children, eight of whom lived with him, and his wife had been seriously ill and collapsed every time there was an alert. Another fire guard who failed to perform his duties just once was fined £20 with five guineas costs. Walter McCabe of Palmer Park Avenue was the ARP Controller for a Reading firm who should have been on duty at 6.30 pm but arrived an hour late, drunk and unable to carry out his duties. He had forgotten he was on duty, gone to the dogs and had a few drinks. Mary Sheehan, who had not paid a fine imposed for absenteeism earlier in the year, pleaded guilty to three further summonses for absenteeism and was sentenced to a month in prison.

A year after the murdered baby had been found in St. Mary's Church porch, a fishing basket floating near Blake's Lock was found to contain a body. The male child was 'wrapped in a piece of sheeting and brown paper, carefully tied with wire string.' There was nothing to identify the child. Death was due either to lack of attention at birth or from the shock of immersion in the river.

Later in the year another baby was found, this time alive in St. Laurence's churchyard. Olive Raine from London pleaded guilty to abandoning her three-week-old son, David, in a manner likely to cause him unnecessary suffering. Her excuse was that she had been evacuated to Bradford-on-Avon and gone home to London to get a pram, failed in her mission and stopped off at Reading on the way back where she wandered about for a while and left the child in the churchyard. When she realised what she had done she returned to find him gone. After spending the night at the railway station she went to the police station to inquire about her baby. She gave an undertaking to move to Brighton and live with her mother and was bound over for a year.

Unrelated, but showing again the dangers of flannelette, a year after a similar tragedy, was the death of 5-year-old Jennifer Hunt of 152 Woodcote Road who died of shock from burns. Her nightdress had caught fire when she went too close to an open fire. Just over a year after the last fatal tree accident, a verdict of accidental death was recorded at the inquest of Gerald Hissey. The 4-year-old had died of his injuries as a result of being struck by a tree during felling operations.

Following the winter coal shortage, residents were warned to buy any type of coal they could get as what they wanted would probably not be available. Again everyone was asked to think before they used power – consumers were not saving enough coal so supplies to industry had fallen by 10 per cent. One easy way to save fuel was the one-pot dinner which, relying on steam, could cook the meat and veg in the same saucepan.

Rats were still a worry. In 1939 and 1940 there had been rat eradication campaigns that had been temporarily successful. Again, everyone was asked to be a 'rat-reporter'. Anyone seeing a rat was asked to complete the form in the newspaper, write to the Public Health Department or phone them, then experts would then track them down. This was another war to win.

The salvage drive arrived days into the New Year and was aimed at business. To provide the striking power for the final 'Victory Blow' and 'Help Speed Production for an Early Victory', the Reading & District Industrial Salvage Group wanted old ledgers, account books, office correspondence files, office records and catalogues.

After a hard day sorting out salvage there were plenty of things to do and see. At the Vaudeville cinema an official government film on the Battle of Britain was showing under the heading *A Page of Glory that is Yours!* More light-hearted was the latest Abbott & Costello film, *Hit the Ice. Aladdin* was still playing at the Palace Theatre and a Grand Dance was held to raise funds for the Red Cross and St. John PoW Fund. For those who wanted to sing there was a free Sunday evening sing-song under the personal patronage of the Mayor. Speaking at the Trade Union Club was the secretary of the London Communist Party, and Ian Mikardo chaired a public meeting about the famine in India. Under a heading that must have confused most – *Britain is Israel* – Mrs Douglas spoke on 'Our National Function'. For those who wanted a flutter there was always greyhound racing.

The housing development of Whitley, of minor national interest in 1943, was debated at length by the council. By a large majority they passed a motion that the survey was 'ill-informed, vague and misleading' and its publication was premature. Councillor McIlroy moved that its publication was damaging to public morale and gave useful information to the enemy. What the Germans would have gained from knowing about living conditions on the estate or that air raid shelters were being used as toilets was not explained. McIlroy went so far as to call Mikardo a lunatic and describe 'parts of the article as a gross libel, absolute nonsense and political claptrap of the worst kind.'

Although no longer headline news, the issue of Whitley did not go away. Indeed, at the end of January the speaker at the Whitley Protest Meeting was Ian Mikardo who invited Councillor McIlroy to be present. His topic was rather pointed: 'My Challenge to Councillor McIlroy.'

One issue highlighted was: lack of provision for young people on the estate. Reading Youth Council made the case for 'improved public services, including an extension to the Community Centre, more buses, more telephone kiosks, a better postal service, and more play apparatus on the "adequate" open spaces'. It was realised that when householders were taken from slums they needed to be educated about their new responsibilities.

The great programme for nationalisation came from a Reading railway worker, Wilf Cannon. His proposals for a state-run railway system were accepted by the Reading Labour Party and taken to the party conference in late 1944 as the 'Reading Resolution', producing 'Labour's commitment to a more radical programme of nationalisation than had previously been anticipated'.

Reading Chamber of Commerce also had weighty matters to discuss: demobilisation and shop hours after the war. They, like many other such groups did not like the government demobilisation plan of first in, first out; they wanted a more planned approach to help the economy. The proposed reduction in shop opening hours was met with opposition from factory representatives.

There was an increasing need for more women to take up employment. Typical was Huntley & Palmers who wanted women over 41 to pack and produce biscuits. In return they offered clean jobs, morning and afternoon breaks, first class recreation facilities, an excellent canteen, and arrangements for friends to work together. Not only would they pay the national biscuit council rate but would provide music to work to and show a film during the dinner hour three times a week. In May they offered the chance to help PoWs by manufacturing and packing Christmas cakes.

In direct competition were the local bus companies. They wanted strong girls who liked an open-air life with plenty of people and movement – the job was bus conductress. At the same time the weight of consignments carried on the buses was reduced because of the volume of passenger traffic and the inability of conductresses to handle heavy consignments: the maximum weight was to be 28 not 56lbs. Also in competition for female employees were the war industries that generally paid more.

There was no sexism in the adverts; it was just that men did certain jobs, even with a war on. Southern Railway in Reading wanted engine cleaners, a job anyone could do but the caveat was that it could lead to being a locomotive fireman, so only boys aged 15½-18 were wanted.

Reading hosted a number of important persons during the year. In January, General Montgomery paid a brief visit during a tour of the Home Counties. He made a special plea for people to give blood to help the wounded. Sir William Beveridge, Hugh Molson MP (Conservative), Miss F. Josephy (Liberal) and Ian Mikardo (Labour) spoke in the Town Hall to open Social

Security week. In the summer Lady Baden-Powell attended a Girl Guides' rally in Palmer Park, and Princess Marie Louise, of German blood, visited the Holt County Girls' School fête. The most important visitor was the Queen who inspected the Army Comforts Depot in St. Mary's Butts for nearly an hour, giving some gramophone records from Princess Elizabeth for dispatch to the troops. She returned days later with the Princess Royal to visit a local ATS Staff College. Later in the year Princess Juliana

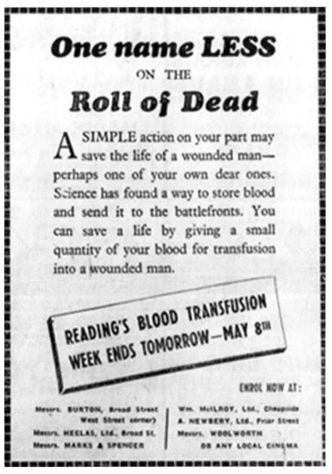

Blood transfusions saved many lives during the war. To ensure a constant supply of fresh blood, the army set up a transfusion service that travelled the country collecting blood.

The Queen and the Princess Royal inspecting a local ATS detachment during a day's visit to them during training.

of Holland paid a surprise visit to the office of the Reading and District Social Services showing particular interest in the Citizen's Advice Bureau.

The 1943 'Baby Boom' continued. Patient admissions to Battle show: 'of 3,138 patients admitted…, 380 went to maternity with 345 deliveries by midwives and 31 by doctors'. The number of births was high for two main reasons. Firstly many were sent to the town to give birth as it was a safe area, and secondly, illegitimacy: something Reading excelled in, with well above the national average rate of one in seven births.

A larger population needed more houses. In March the council took the first steps to provide new homes after the war by compulsorily purchasing plots of land abutting Northumberland Avenue.

Randomly in May there were convictions for serious sex offences – a very rare occurrence. Kenneth Roberts, a merchant seaman, was bound on probation for two years charged with an offence against a 13-year-old girl. Victor Morris, a soldier, pleaded guilty to an offence against a girl over 13 and under 16; they were determined to get married when the law allowed it. He received a six month sentence. Victor James pleaded guilty to having committed a grave offence against his daughter, then under the age of 16, on a number of occasions. The judge sentenced him to four years' penal servitude.

In the same assizes, a paratrooper sergeant pleaded not guilty to the manslaughter of Pilot Officer Luckett. He was found guilty with a recommendation because of his good civilian and military character and bound over on probation for two years. Luckett had his arms around the paratrooper's wife and fell when hit and cracked his skull.

Once again people were advised to have a 'Staycation'. 'Lend a Hand on the Land' was one option the government wanted as many people as possible to choose: 'Spend your holiday at a farm camp and do your bit to safeguard our country against the food shortages facing the world.' With pay at 1s an hour minimum, each volunteer needed to work 28 hours to pay for their accommodation.

For those staying at home, there was always a lot to do in, on and around the Thames. Maynard's river trips were popular and inexpensive, a return to Sonning with thirty minutes ashore was 1s 6d. For those wanting to venture further there were three afternoon trips a week to Goring. Across the borough and beyond there were garden fêtes, open air political meetings, regular evening dances, swimming galas, athletic events, a concert in the Town Hall featuring the New London Orchestra, and a whole week of open-air entertainment at Caversham Court in late August.

To tempt holidaymakers to stay in Reading events were held throughout the week. Typically, a Grand Hospital Carnival was held midweek in Sol Joel Park to raise money for the Royal Berks. It was a very busy afternoon and evening with three bands performing, a horticultural show and sale of produce, athletics, boxing, PT, dancing displays, a dog show, darts tournament, dancing and a Punch & Judy. It advertised picnic teas and that tea was provided but visitors were advised to bring their own cup or jug and food owing to rationing regulations. Such events continued in to early autumn with the Industrial Fire Service and ARP Rally in the Stadium, Oxford Road, on 3 September, the fifth anniversary of the start of the war.

With the salvage drive barely over, Reading was once again asked to dig deep. Another National Savings Week was to be held in June: Salute the Soldier, with a target of £1,000,000, had £348,000 promised before it officially started. The plans to raise money were novel: a small army of parachutists hanging from buildings round the town, a silhouette model soldier in the GWR station, a sign to indicate how much had been collected outside Heelas' and a miniature of the Trafalgar Square platform in Market Place, with a speaker each day at 3pm and a band. The Deputy Mayor also wanted a British Restaurant there to make it a focal point for the week. Quoting last year's total for Wings Week, the Mayor asked Reading to raise £1,500,000. A fortnight after it began the total was £1,414,579.

The week opened in King's Meadow following a parade, with displays and events in parks across the town, including an 89-piece American army band. In the Town Hall Lord Mottisone opened an exhibition: 'The History of the British Soldier'. It was a tribute to the men and women of the army and ATS, illustrated with large coloured photographs depicting the development of the army, including up-to-date photographs of Dunkirk, North Africa and Italy. What probably appealed to the majority were the equipment and weapons on display.

During the week, the Allies invaded France. Shortly after the news, a service of prayer and dedication was held at St. Laurence's church, attended by a congregation of several hundred people. Throughout the day there was a steady stream of people entering the church to pray. 'Prayers were offered for the services, leaders and others.'

The first recorded local death of the invasion was Lieutenant Hinton of Southampton Street.

As a result of the invasion there was an urgent demand for reading material for the troops. For some unexplained reason

There was no advertising authority to check adverts during the war. This ad speaks for itself on a number of levels and was not viewed as anything but humorous and informative.

every local authority in Berkshire except Reading was taking part. The books were to be collected by children who were the 'Berkshire Book Recovery Army'. They were rewarded with badges and a rank according to the number of books they handed in. For 25 books they became a sergeant, for 50 a captain, 150 made them a general and 250 a field marshal. Their motto was 'Clear out every book and magazine'.

Berkshire was home to many of the troops who would form the vanguard of the D-Day landings. Margaret Fairburn recalled 6 June: her family stood on their back lawn in Beech Lane, Earley and 'watched a huge fleet of planes towing gliders filled with soldiers literally filling the sky, the ground beneath our feet throbbing'.

In a sure sign that the danger of air attack was over, firewatchers were asked to hand in their helmets and eyeshades, but were allowed to keep their armlets. However, the danger was not over, the next attacks were by rocket. Although targeted against London, they often went off course, with one descending into 'a field at the top of Beech Lane, just behind the farmhouse which now houses the Town Council offices, damaging the chimneystacks. There were some broken windows and a few cuts, and a big crater [that was] almost immediately cordoned off by the American Army.' The paper reported that there was no hole, just the wreckage of the 'plane' and that Mrs Austin's cuts needed hospital treatment. Clive Rowden was standing in Meadow Road with his siblings when he heard the V1 coming towards him. Overhead the engine cut out and they all fell to the ground. Mrs West recalled the drone of the engine as it flew overhead, then silence, followed by an explosion. It is recorded the there was a casualty: a cow was blown up. The V1 rocket on 19 June was the final enemy attack on the town.

In the same edition of the paper was the story of a local pilot. Flight Lieutenant Arthur Moore of 25 Cressingham Road had become an ace, having shot down five V1s, three in one day, and a Messerschmitt ME 109 over France just weeks before. In March 1945 he was awarded a bar to his DFC.

There was a further wave of evacuees as a result of the flying bombs. With the over-running of the flying bombs' fixed bases, the evacuees once again left, only to return when the Germans launched V2 rocket attacks.

Local evacuees also began returning. In August, the Lund-Yates of Blenheim Road, Caversham, were reunited with their three children, Allan, aged 18, Maureen, aged 14, and Michael, 10. They had left for America in late 1940.

The war in Italy was overshadowed by the battles in France but there were many Reading men fighting there, as *The Standard* showed with an article on CSM Frederick Josey of Hazel Court. He had been abroad since spring 1942, spending a year in Irak (sic), followed by fighting in Sicily and Italy. He was promoted in the field at Anzio to RSM.

Although Italy was now fighting with the Allies, there were still many Italian PoWs in the area. As they were PoWs, any correspondence had to go through the mail to be checked. Mrs Mann, of 93 Castle Street, was separated from her husband and had struck up a correspondence with a PoW she had met. For writing to him through unofficial channels she was fined £5, with four weeks to pay, with the alternative of a month's imprisonment.

Among the stories about the exploits of local men was a small piece on a woman. ACW1 Evelyn Nicholls of 61 Kingsbridge Road was mentioned in despatches by her commanding officer for 'devotion to duty'. She was 22 years old and had worked for Heelas Ltd before joining the RAF. For some reason, the death of a female Air Transport Auxiliary pilot did not rate a space in the Roll of Honour, even though she had died on duty. F/Captain the Hon. Mrs Margaret Fairweather of Kidmore End died from injuries when her plane crashed on the way to Scotland.

Devotion to duty was needed as the Mayoress asked the women of Reading and anyone else who had the time to sell flags on Sailor's Flag Day: target £1,000. At the same time there were appeals for clean second-hand clothing in a reasonable state of repair for persons who had lost their belongings in the latest wave of raids.

The Royal Berks was very busy during the year, taking 3,322 X-rays and performing 676 operations. Out-patients dealt with 3,942 accident cases and there were 1,260 attendances at the out-patient clinic.

During the year the town suffered a major outbreak of scabies. 'Between the School Clinic, Battle and six other dedicated clinics set up in the town's First Aid Posts, nearly 1,500 cases of scabies were reported.'

Battle Hospital dealt with men from all three services but not those who had been wounded. The men were sent because of accidents, hernias or varicose veins. 'Convoys would come up from Haslar Naval Hospital, as many as 60 patients, usually with gastric problems.' Not all were genuinely ill; some were malingering for early release. Nurse Adler worked in the ward and recalled the cure for time-wasters: 'a diet of milk 1 oz every two hours.'

The Royal Berks was also affected by the military, with civilian admissions restricted to cope with the expected number of invasion casualties; only urgent civilian cases were admitted. As a result, by the end of the year nearly 800 people were waiting for operations along with 490 tonsil cases. Of the 700 servicemen admitted during the year, only a few were casualties of the landings. The Royal Berks contribution was to send large amounts of blood to the military hospitals in Portsmouth, Southampton and Winchester.

Battle ran a nursery. During the year it admitted 15 destitute mothers (13 evacuees, 2 from Reading) and their illegitimate children. Unfortunately some children were living there permanently.

With black-out being replaced by dim-out – equivalent light to the moon, it meant that church services could return to pre-war times. The proviso was that in the case of an air raid, blackout conditions would apply.

The standing down of the Home Guard was a certain sign of impending victory. The Royal Berkshire Regiment journal wrote a fittingly eloquent epitaph. 'They were never called upon to function in their true role…the Home Guard must have caused the German General Staff very largely to have recast their invasion plans…and even with shotguns and petrol and petrol bottles…would have left their teeth marks on the enemy…And now they will fade away… *Sic transit Gloria mundi.*' It was marked in Reading with a big parade, followed by special services at local churches and for some units a Stand Down dinner. A lucky few were selected to represent the Berkshire Home Guard at the Standing Down parade at Hyde Park where they marched past the King.

Although the war was showing signs of ending, the number of troops being sent overseas was still increasing. With 100 million books collected just weeks earlier, Churchill was asking for more.

The Berkshire County Bowling Association were so confident that the war would end in 1945 they decided to return to pre-war conditions. If it did not finish in 1945, they agreed they would continue the Red Cross competition.

Numbers of PoWs began arriving home. School friends Charles Prior and Arthur Benham, of numbers 10 and 13 Auckland Road, escaped from their Italian PoW camp and arrived home unexpectedly at the end of September. Their trip had taken nine months, during which time they had been helped by Italian farmers and worked with the partisans in the mountains. A week later Mrs Powell of 210 Cranbury Road received a letter from her son Herbert saying that he had successfully escaped in Italy. Petty Officer Martin had spent his leave at home in Caversham; he too had successfully escaped from the Germans in Italy three times since April.

With the night drawing in there was no shortage of entertainment to be had. There were numerous films to choose from, and for those with a terpsichorean bent there were no end of dance classes and balls. Amusingly, tucked in amongst the announcements was a small advert: PAINFUL FEET? If so, consult M.E. Gray, chiropodist and shoe fitter.

To enjoy such pastimes required public transport. For no reason that was explained after years of buses not running late, suddenly at the end of October the last bus would run 30 minutes later than usual, but there was no change to Sunday travel.

Poppy Day collections it was hoped would reach £3,500, £500 more

Private Dennis Jennings, whose parents lived at 32 Stanley Street, and attended Buckingham Palace after the war to collect their son's bravery medal, won on 16 May 1944 in Italy. He had been killed in action on 8 June the same year.

than 1943. This was not to be: the total at the start of December was less than the previous year, at £2,784 3s 8d. Again there was no official Armistice Day commemoration, but wreaths were laid at the war memorial.

There were many honours given towards the end of the year: Squadron Leader Rippingdale was awarded the DSO, Lieutenant Commander Brown of Talfourd Avenue the DSC, Flying Officer Bluring of Addington Road the DFC, Petty Officer Landon of Oxford Road the DSM, Sergeant Soames the DFM, Able Seaman Brooker was Mentioned in Despatches and Lieutenant Colonel Field, RSM Ball, Major Cockburn and CSM White were all awarded the OBE. Squadron Leader Williams of 105 Kenilworth Avenue led a squadron of bombers which helped sink the German battleship *Tirpitz*; he did not receive a medal but Major Vanderpump did for being a member of the Home Guard.

In the run up to Christmas the demand for money continued and in early December the Red Cross ran a Billiards and Snooker Week. Money raised was to go to PoWs and the wounded. Spare cash was wanted by the government for National Savings. As an aid to further savings it was reported that during the past year – ended 30 September – Reading had saved £3,221,753, an increase of £216,916 on the previous year.

Again there was limited public transport over the Christmas holiday and limited shopping opportunities. Reading Chamber of Commerce recommended traders closed as usual on the Wednesday afternoon before Christmas and all day between 25 to 27 December, except for food. Strangely, the Co-op, unable to deliver bread between 23 to 27 December, delivered milk on Christmas Day but not Boxing Day.

Reading had a final part to play in the evacuee story. In mid-December 4,000 evacuee children, many accompanied by their mothers, spent a night in the town on their return journey; they had been living in Cornwall, Devon and Wales. Reading was also helping those who returned to bombed homes. The town had taken Lewisham under its wing where it was reported that 1,129 houses had been completely destroyed; 1,153 were uninhabitable,

5,305 were seriously damaged and a further 55,303 were partially damaged. Apart from money, the public were asked to donate household items such as ornaments, pictures, crockery, toys, furniture, kitchen equipment, and general odds and ends.

At the final Quarter Sessions of the year, the Chief Constable reported an increase in burglary/housebreaking and juvenile crime. Sadly there had also been an increase in road traffic accidents and deaths: an increase of 13 killed and 145 injured.

The first public expressions of the season came from the Air Training Corps. They wished all ex-cadets 'Good Luck and Safe Landings for 1945'. This was followed by H. Samuel, the Empire's largest jeweller, and the Reading Co-op, that hoped for brighter times in the New Year. Corona drinks cleverly expressed their wish for business as greetings: 'Speed the time we can all spend Christmas in the good old-fashioned way, and the

By Christmas it was clear that the war would not last that much longer, and Christmas greetings for victory were more realistic than in previous years.

"Corona" man once more brings these delightful drinks right to your door.' Langston & Sons sent Christmas greetings, hoping that 1945 would bring Happiness and Victory, and Aldridge's in Friar Street headed their greeting, 'To a Victory Christmas'.

There was a choice of activities to make the season jollier. The Town Hall hosted a Grand Christmas Ball on 22 December with another on Boxing Night. Across town there was a dance at the Tilehurst Road Hall on 23 December. The Airborne Forces Security Fund advertised a Grand Cinderella Ball and Cabaret on 27 December, and in the large Town Hall there was a New Year's Eve Dance. For those who could not get enough dancing, it was available every night at the Olympia. More passive folk could enjoy one of the many films available, of which the most famous was *Dumbo*.

Few gifts were advertised. Gift tokens or Savings Stamps seemed to be the best choice.

The leader writer of *The Standard* noted, in the issue before Christmas, that 'we are passing through tremendous and terrible times…we are fighting…to save civilisation…our particular civilisation…we must make it our business to see that it is worth all that is being done to save it.'

It was another stay-at-home Christmas for most, and although it was the sixth of the war, there had been plenty of good things to eat. There were numerous children's parties and the Mayor and Mayoress spent the day visiting hospitals and other institutions. Wounded service men and women were given Christmas stockings containing two books or magazines, two writing pads, envelopes, twenty cigarettes, jam, apple, pencil, razorblades, shaving soap, matches and a pot of ink. The children of employees of Miles Aircraft did especially well. At their party were eight giant Christmas cakes, hundreds of fairy cakes, chocolate biscuits and jellies. How the company managed to get all the ingredients was not disclosed. Each child also received, from Father Christmas, an apple, a bag of sweets and a threepenny piece.

At the end of the year the papers reported divorces and bicycle thefts. There was the constant demand not to use electricity at certain times of the day, a golden wedding to celebrate, how the town had spent Christmas, a review of the year and the story of Mary Gollop of 9 Belle Vue Terrace. At the age of 43, she had just given birth to her fifteenth child, of which fourteen were alive. She had become a grandmother at the age of 35.

The front page classified ads contained deaths on active service, some recording more than one loss: Clarke. – Sacred to the memory of my two dear youngest sons, Petty Officer Phillip James, and Eric Walter, R.N., who made the supreme sacrifice, December 18, 1940, and March 9, 1943. Some included a short verse, others a comment. The parents and sisters of Private Harrington of 23 Caroline Street concluded their entry with a simple statement about their son: 'To the world he was one, To us, all the world.' A few pages further in was the final Roll of Honour for 1944 which reported the death of Able Seaman Tony Griffin of 50 Culver Lane, followed by a short piece on the four healthy sons of Mr and Mrs Overson of 23 The Grove, all serving their country.

Milward's shoe shops finished with an advert containing the statement that was probably on most people's minds: '1945, A New Year... and each day is one day nearer Peace.'

CHAPTER SEVEN

1945

The year started with a warning. 'During exceptionally cold or foggy weather increased consumption of electricity and gas puts a severe burden on plant capacity and labour supply, which are already strained by wartime production needs. The strain as regards electricity is especially acute between 8 am and 10 am, so PLEASE cut your consumption as much as possible.'

Captain W. Davis DSC presented a Nazi ensign taken from an E-Boat by HMS Garth during the Allied assault on Walcheren to the Mayor. What happened to it after the handover is unclear.

This was followed by an SOS! Reading Co-operative Society was short of milk bottles. The leader writer of *The Standard* was not exactly positive about the coming year, describing it as 'the beginning again of all the phases through which we pass in endless repetition'. The good news was that it was sale time, although there was not much available.

After the classifieds came the Roll of Honour, with twelve deaths in the Royal Berkshire Regiment and the Ox & Bucks Light Infantry and an obituary for two local men. Sapper Beckford of 85 Ashburton Road had been killed on 21 December clearing mines on the south coast. He was buried at Reading Cemetery. Royal Marine Grant from Dunsden had been killed by enemy air action. Just a few pages on was a Reading family's admirable record of four smiling sons all doing their bit. This was trumped a week later by the Knight family of Mount Street with five sons, two sons-in-law and a grandson serving.

The New Year's honours list contained many locals: local MP Dr Howitt was knighted, Mr H. Palmer received the MBE, Lieutenant Woodeson, RN, was awarded the DSC, Flight Lieutenant Fifield was awarded the DFC, Lieutenant Tarrant of 299 Oxford Road was awarded the MC, Sergeant Squelch and Lance-Corporal Wickens of 49 Francis Street received the BEM as did Sergeant Davies; Able Seaman Gilbert Breadmore of 175 Thirlmere Avenue was mentioned in despatches, he was serving in X-craft midget submarines.

There were photos of Christmas weddings and a round-up of the cases heard in court. Among the minor cases was stealing from grandfather, leaving the mines to enlist, and stealing from

Captain Price was killed on 14 February 1945 in the fighting in Germany while serving with the Royal Berkshire Regiment. A married man, he had lived at 17 Mansfield Road.

The House family were proud to have four sons serving in the army and all still alive in early 1945. From the left, Stanley, the eldest, serving with the Signals, Fred, a Sergeant Gunner in the artillery, Dennis, a craftsman in the REME, and 18-year-old Bob who was in the Catering Corps.

a postal packet. One was of considerable importance: stealing food and alcohol from GWR wagons. Sidney Cannon of 153 Gosbrook Road, Leonard Andrews of 44 Cardiff Road (his father pleaded guilty as an accessory after the fact concerning his son's thefts), Eric Bartlett of 26 Letcombe Street and Sidney Saunders of 52 Valentine Crescent all pleaded guilty to stealing and/or receiving dozens of bottles of whisky, wines and liqueurs, cartons of Christmas puddings, and several packing cases of margarine and chocolate. Cannon was sent to prison for four months on the first charge and four months and three months imprisonment respectively on the second and subsequent charges, the sentences to run concurrently; Bartlett received two sentences of two months' imprisonment to run concurrently; Saunders was sentenced to two months imprisonment on each charge, the sentences to run concurrently; Andrews was given three sentences of three months to run concurrently, his father was fined just £10. Gwyn Rees, Eleanor West and James Cannon were found guilty of receiving stolen goods but were dealt with very leniently.

Following the negative came two positive stories. The first was that of Petty Officer Norris of 26 Callington Road and his experiences during combined operations in Albania.

In just twenty-four hours he led the capture of a heavily-armed enemy ferry, was wounded, narrowly escaped drowning, and arranged the surrender of the enemy craft. The second story was of 2-year-old John Wyatt, who was critically ill in the Royal Berks suffering from coeliac disease. He refused to take the dehydrated bananas supplied. Records showed that a patient being treated in the Middle East responded positively to fresh bananas; within a day an appeal for help through the RAF Technical Training Command HQ resulted in fresh bananas being delivered. As a result he made a good recovery.

In 1945, Sergeant E. Dance of the WAAF completed five years service. She came from Woodley.

An incredible story was revealed about an 80-year-old Reading man in Burma. Ex-Sergeant-Major Watts was the only Englishman to remain in central Burma throughout the Japanese occupation. After being invalided out of the army he had lived in Burma with his Burmese wife and become the head man of the village. Staying after the invasion when he could have escaped, he grew a long white beard to deceive the Japanese. This was the first news his elder brother had received about him since 1939.

The same issue of the paper reported the 100th birthday of Mrs Sarah Frost, whose mother, also a Reading native, lived to 102. A few weeks later Mrs Sarah Drew celebrated her 101st birthday; she was still taking short walks and attended church every Sunday.

It was a cold winter. So cold that the lakes in the university froze over enabling people to skate and toboggan on the surface. Once again, coal supplies were short with households being restricted to fifteen hundredweight for a three month period.

One very different story that emerged as the Pacific war was winding down was that of RSM Watts, an ex-Berkshire Regiment soldier. He had stayed on in Burma when he completed his service and married a local woman. Throughout the war he had helped the Allies with information about the Japanese troops in the area.

Exotic fruit was very scarce, so much so that its arrival in the area was put on the front page in the classifieds. Naturally its purchase was controlled. In mid-February, for the first time in months Reading received lemons, oranges and marmalade oranges. For some children it was the first time they had seen such fruit other than in a picture. A month later Reading received another consignment of oranges and some grapefruit and a week later another consignment of lemons.

In the Great War, illegitimate births had mostly been covered up, some babies had even been killed. By 1939 attitudes had changed: it was still frowned upon but was not the great shame of the previous war. The illegitimacy 'rate in Reading was considerably above that for England and Wales. This is not surprising considering the large numbers of evacuated persons, war-workers, and troops, torn from their normal surroundings and restricting influences, who found themselves in Reading. The peak rate in Reading was reached in 1945 when for every six legitimate births there was one illegitimate.' Possibly coincidentally, in February, the social services held a public meeting for parents on sex education, and in March a large advert highlighted VD, a 'Shadow on Health', explaining what it was, how it was caught, its effects, and where and how it could be treated.

With resources short, Social Services could not protect all the town's children. March saw the prosecution of Beatrice Lennington and James Waldron in what was described as one of the worst cases of child neglect to come before the bench. They pleaded not guilty to causing by wilful neglect unnecessary suffering and injury to the health to their six children aged between 12 months and 8 years. All six slept in one room on two beds, the three eldest children in a single bed, the rest shared the double bed. Living conditions were appalling, there was virtually no food and the children who were dirty and verminous lacked shoes and socks. The youngest child had been severely burned when its pram had been accidentally set on fire by the 3-year-old son. A litany of neglect was paraded before the bench and Lennington was sentenced to six months and Waldron fined £20.

For the third time in three years another child was found abandoned. In March an 18-month-old girl was found in the cloakroom of the Oatsheaf Hotel in Broad Street. There were no clues as to her identity a week after she was found.

In the same week a dead baby was found in an alley from Cranbourne Gardens to Ringwood Road. The unclothed body was believed to have been abandoned at birth. Her death had been caused by lack of attention.

They were not the only children to die in March. Two-year-old Judy Stansell died after falling out of an upstairs window; and a 5-month-old baby boy died in hospital a month after he had swallowed a safety pin. Although the pin had been safely removed he died from peritonitis.

In February, the town had a surprise visitor. On his way back to London from Yalta, Winston Churchill stopped at the Great Western Hotel. News of his presence spread quickly and when he left thirty minutes later there were crowds lining the pavement to see him.

Although the war in Europe was drawing to a close, there was still a need for men to join the army. Registering for the draft continued unabated and in March young men born between 1 April and 30 June 1927 were deemed to have joined the forces unless unfit or in protected employment. They were mostly destined not to fight but garrison enemy territory and the empire.

Like the standing down of the Home Guard, a clear sign that the European War really was ending was found in the classifieds. In early March, Berkshire County Council advertised surplus civil defence vehicles for sale.

Corporal K. Belsham of 4 Milton Road was in the papers for his 'gallant and distinguished services in Italy'.

But there was no let-up in the casualties. The Roll of Honour not only included those recently killed but those who had been missing for some time and now presumed to be dead.

By the end of March, the V2 rocket campaign had ceased and almost immediately evacuees returned home. Then, with the European war over, the remaining evacuees quickly left Reading, leaving behind only homeless children and the aged. 'Between January and September 1945 the total population of the town fell by just over nineteen thousand, but it was still some nineteen thousand more than in June 1939.' By the end of the year there were few evacuees and refugees in the town and with the ending of the war the number of war workers fell rapidly. But not all left: a year later 150 families had requested to be placed on the Corporation housing list rather than return home.

Back in October, the time of the last bus had been put back, now in March they were able to revise the timetable, include additional evening services and introduce new services. This was to include both local and longer distance services; yet another sign of peace coming.

In March came news of a wedding. There had been many weddings of American servicemen to local women but this was the first between a Reading soldier and a Dutch woman, and almost certainly the first in the British Liberation Army. Corporal Benham of 24 Queen's Road married Anna Koopmans at the beginning of May. Coincidentally, his younger brother had just married an American he met while stationed in the States, and

It was to be expected that British soldiers in liberated countries would have some form of relationship with the female public and that some would get married. The first Reading man to succumb was Corporal Maurice Benham of 24 Queen's Road. He married a Dutch woman.

was honeymooning at the time. Amusingly the Palace Theatre was running a farce called *Is your Honeymoon really necessary?*

The coming of the end of the war must have been very obvious: at the end of March, C. Simms of 39 Surrey Road suggested that a giant bonfire should be built in Reading's biggest park, fenced off to stop premature lighting, ready for the big day as a prelude to the victory march when Japan was defeated.

As the Allied troops advanced into Germany, they liberated PoWs, some of who had been captive since 1939. Two men captured in 1940 returned home in early April. Corporal Wyatt of 6 Gloucester Road was liberated by American troops and quickly put on a plane home. Trooper Addis of 913 Oxford Road was liberated by Russians and returned home to his wife and a son he had never met. Glider pilot Staff Sergeant Payton of Shinfield arrived home at the end of April. He had been in the army since 1939 but had only been a PoW since September 1944 when he was captured at Arnhem.

Even though the end of the war was in sight there was still a need for the land girls to keep working. It would be some time before all the men had been demobbed and could return to their employment on the land. This is a group of Land Girls somewhere in Berkshire in 1944.

As the war drew to a close, many men were liberated from PoW camps and returned home, sometimes to children they had never met. This is Corporal A. Prior meeting his daughter for the first time.

Another released PoW was Fusilier Albert Provins of 1 Francis Street, who had spent the whole of his captivity in an Austrian hospital. He was captured in Italy in December 1944 and released as the war ended.

In the Far East, Private Slade arrived from Manila where he had been liberated by American troops. He had survived four years in Japanese PoW camps, including working on the infamous railway in Thailand.

While welcoming home PoWs, the town paid tribute to the late President Roosevelt; flags were flown at half-mast from all public buildings, churches and many other premises. The Mayor sent a telegram to the White House expressing the town's grief over the loss of a great American. He also telegraphed the Mayor of Reading, Pennsylvania, sending the town's condolences on their loss of a great president. Memorial services were held in many churches and chapels.

Alongside the column on President Roosevelt's death were three local fatalities; all from uncertain causes. It was thought

Over the course of the war there had been many stories of friends and brothers meeting in unlikely circumstances. Randomly, two school friends and members of Battle Athletic Football Club met in the Pacific while on leave.

that Frank Allen of Ashburton Road had an epileptic fit while fishing and fell into the Kennet. Strong swimmer William Warwick's drowning while swimming in the Thames was recorded as accidental, while the suspicious death of landlord William Grapel was not solved. He had been hit by a heavy vehicle but there were no witnesses; the coroner left the verdict open as to the cause of his injuries.

Many must have pondered on what victory would mean and entail. Days before VE-Day, it was explained by the Corona drinks company: victory meant that Corona would be 'delivered again to your door'. Brooke Bond told residents that among the many benefits of the freedom from control would be that they would be able to get as much of the brand of tea they preferred. What it did not mean was that people were free to go on holiday whenever they wanted. People were asked to go away only during June, September and October, to ease the load on the railways.

Victory would certainly reduce the numbers in the Roll of Honour and increase the number of returned PoWs. In the week before the end of the war in Europe there were no local deaths, just two wounded, but the following week's paper carried details of the death of the only son of Mr and Mrs Owen of 15 Beecham Road; he had been killed in action in Italy on 3 March. A week later Mrs Watkins of 45 Newport Road learned of the death of her husband on 1 May; he had been expected home on leave in June.

This was followed a week later by the death of Sapper Findlay of The World Turned Upside Down on Basingstoke Road. A released PoW, the plane bringing him home crashed on 6 May killing all thirty ex-PoWs and the four crew. Ex-PoW James Allen of 57 Belmont Road died at Battle Hospital after a long illness. He had escaped to Switzerland from where he had been repatriated

Able Seaman Harold Anscomb, of Meadow Road, survived the bombing and sinking of his ship, HMS Afridi, off the Norwegian coast on 2 May. He died on 9 April 1945 and is buried in Bari War Cemetery in Italy.

Although the war was winding down, aircrew especially went missing on operations. Mr and Mrs Farnbank of 122 Whitley Street were lucky parents. Their son had been missing for some time when news arrived that he was alive.

Trooper Frederick Bayliss, serving with 2 Fife and Forfar Yeomanry, Royal Armoured Corps, died in the last weeks of the war. He was killed in action on 19 April 1945, at Rottorf, and is buried in Becklingen War Cemetery.

ill. On 17 May, Sergeant Smith of 16 Lorne Street died in a flying accident and on VE-Day 2, 25 June, Sergeant R. Seymour of 31 Surrey Road also died in a plane crash.

More positively, in the days leading up to VE-Day, thirteen men returned home from PoW camps, one of whom had attempted to escape on six occasions.

The lifting of some aspects of censorship meant the return of weather reports in the daily papers. It also allowed the role of the BBC's monitoring service in Caversham to be told. It employed hundreds of workers of many nationalities, some of whom spoke and wrote as many as eight languages. Before the German surrender they were listening to about 1¼ million words a day in thirty-two languages, transcribing 300,000 words a day into English. It was only natural that the monitoring centre at Caversham Park was the first place to hear about the German surrender.

Four days earlier the government had sent out guidelines on how the victory should be celebrated if Germany surrendered unconditionally. The day of cessation of organised resistance was to be VE-Day and the next day would be a public holiday. Arrangements for reporting the end of the war and the council attending a church service were complicated by the potential time of the announcement. Regardless, there was a statement as to the declaration of victory from outside the Town Hall.

VE-Day, 8 May, was a national holiday. Reading celebrated with bonfires (often burning a Hitler effigy), dancing in the streets, fireworks, church bells and street parties. In Armour Hill about forty children were entertained at a victory party held at number 26, the home of Mr and Mrs S. Tanner, who

The crowd assembled to listen to the broadcast about the end of the war was large; this is just a section of it.

with Mrs Cronin arranged a tea and sports with savings stamps as prizes. Each child was presented with a souvenir beaker made by Mr Tanner Jr.

Margaret Fairburn was at school and everyone was sent home. As she cycled home she was astonished 'to see every house (including hers), draped with allied flags. The next day there was a huge bonfire lit at the junction of Beech Lane and Wilderness Road.'

The vicar of Sonning noted that in the village, 'VE day was celebrated not only by a fine display of bunting, bonfires, rockets and the pealing of the church bells but also by a short but heartfelt Service of Praise at 8 am when the church was nearly filled by a congregation which sang the glad hymns with real fervour.'

Lighting restrictions were lifted as there was no chance of an air raid. Many buildings were floodlit. Berkshire Highways Commission reimposed the partial blackout in July to save money and wanted it to continue until 1 September. Although voted down by the Town Council it stayed in place. The next argument was whether to turn the lights off at midnight, which the council won.

The two boys born that day in the Dellwood Maternity Home were called Victor. Two girls were also born on 8 May at the Grove Maternity Home; their names were not recorded in the paper.

VE-Day got two young railway firemen into trouble. William Hughes and John Davies, both of 118 Chatham Street appeared in court for stealing detonators belonging to the GWR. They had used them for fireworks in a bonfire. After smashing the glass in a street sign, Kenneth Thorngate, serving in the Royal Navy, was arrested and fined 10s. His excuse was that he had been drinking, fighting with an American soldier and lost his temper. He had been at sea for three months and was making up for what he did not see on VE-Day.

The end of the war with Japan often brought news about men missing for some considerable time, or who had been a PoW, but little had been heard from them. Warrant Officer F. Willis' wife of 74 Water Road received notification after the war that her husband had died in a PoW camp in Borneo on 5 February 1945 in Java.

Unknowingly, the day before VE-Day was selected as the date for the publication of the register of parliamentary electors. The nation was going to the polls in the same way it had at the end of the Great War. In June the papers carried pieces on the local candidates across Reading and Berkshire. There were three candidates for Reading: the ex-Mayor was running as the National candidate, a continuation of the wartime coalition, in reality he was a conservative, Flight-Lieutenant

Tronchin-James was representing the Liberal Party, and Ian
Mikardo was the Labour candidate. Voting was not until 5 July
but because of the overseas service vote the result would not
be known until 26 July. The turnout was one of the heaviest on
record with a steady flow of voters throughout the day. Many
London evacuees, placed on Reading's electoral roll during the
war, returned to the town to vote. One man from Hammersmith
travelled on a packed midnight train and was the first to vote;
he immediately caught a train home after voting. The Labour
candidate, Ian Mikardo, was elected the new member for Reading with a 6,390 majority, and readers of *The Standard* were told

*Although she was 101, Mrs Drew of 32 Junction Road went to vote in the general
election.*

they wouldn't have long to wait before Corona deliveries began again. Weeks later, Labour gained thirteen of the eighteen vacant council seats.

Sunday, 13 May, as requested by the King, was Thanksgiving Sunday. It was marked by church services in the morning and a parade of service units, Home Guard and Civil Defence personnel. At 8pm an open-air service was held in Forbury Gardens. Reading's Victory Parade 'surpassed anything of the kind that had ever taken place in the borough... people in thousands filled the streets to watch the men and women of all services go by, and filled the churches to take part in the special services.'

After VE Day, notifications of deaths in Europe continued as the situation became clearer. One death was that of Flight Lieutenant Douglas Wix DFC, a married man; he had died on operations a month before the end of the European war.

The papers also reported those who had been wounded in the closing days of the fighting in Germany. Paratrooper H. Willis was wounded in March.

A further day's holiday was granted on 25 June for all Reading schools. It was called VE2 Day and all businesses were urged to close as well. There was a programme of events in Palmer Park, opened by the Mayor, and a parade of decorated vehicles through the town with no motorised entries due to fuel rationing. Activities in the park included the standard athletics competition and fancy dress parade but more intriguing was the ladies' ankle competition. Three events not to miss were Harry Benet's Circus horses and ponies, a bicycle polo match, and the novelty dog show which had some clever and humorous performances. Later in the evening there was community singing, the massed bands of the Army Technical School and a boxing tournament. It was reputed to be the largest crowd ever seen attending celebrations in the park.

The merriment was not confined to Palmer Park. There was dancing at the Forbury Pleasure Grounds, at the Thames-side Promenade the Miles Aircraft Band gave a concert, and in Prospect Park the Salvation Army band played.

Among the returning PoWs was a Reading family. Mr and Mrs King and their 10-year-old son had been in captivity since the German occupation of Jersey in 1940.

Not everyone was celebrating. Most cases at the Berkshire Summer Assizes were bigamy, with the judge commenting that 'it seems in this county that bigamy is not a crime.' He sentenced three men and three women to jail for between four months and a year. A month later charges were brought against eleven youths, two aged 18 and

Although the war in Europe had finished, there was still fighting in the Pacific. One casualty was First Class Stoker Dennis Clarke of 'Tralee', Loddon Bridge Road. He was reported missing, presumed killed, in the last months of the war.

nine under 16. They had been stealing cars for fun. The Chief Constable reported that there had been an increase in burglary/housebreaking compared to the same quarter in 1944 but there had been a decrease in fatalities and injuries on the road.

The horrors of Belsen were reported through the eyes of a local man, Major St. Claire Stewart, son-in-law of a former Mayor of Wokingham. It was a harrowing account that described the smell, squalor, apathy and acceptance of death by the inmates. There were decomposing naked bodies of men, women and children dumped in a pile. Further inside he saw a pile of dead bodies 80 by 30 yards about three feet high, and nearby were a group sitting down cooking a potato in a fire or lying in the sun.

Later in the year, an unnamed ex-PoW of the Japanese described his harrowing experiences, followed by the story of Ronald Absolom of 30 Brisbane Street and how he escaped being shot by the Japanese during his captivity.

There was still an urgent need for blood. As casualties returned to the country from Europe and with the war continued in the east, large numbers of casualties arrived at Battle Hospital. The Army Blood Transfusion service travelled around collecting blood but only came to large areas such as Reading. To make sure of volunteers from outside the town, villagers were asked to make an appointment to give blood on Tuesday or Friday afternoons at The Royal Berks.

Reading's hospitals had worked hard, even though short staffed, to provide essential services. The draft report of surveys completed nationally during 1943, published during the year, must have been heartbreaking reading for some staff, but it did point the way forward. The Royal Berks buildings were noted to be 'antiquated and inadequate (with the exception of the new Nuffield Block and the Pathological Department)'. Battle Hospital was described as not being up to the standards of modern hospitals and it had to rely on specialist staff from the Royal Berks where there were some good men on the staff but posts were not always held by those most suited. Neither hospital was rated adequate for the population.

As the war drew to a close many locals were honoured for their efforts. These are just a selection. Able Seaman Douglas Bruce-Jones of 27 Culver Lane, a naval diver, aged only 18, was awarded the BEM for 'daring and unsurpassed courage' while clearing Europe's ports. Private Rogers of 11 Selbourne Gardens received the MM, and 23-year-old Major Excell of 68 Shinfield Road was awarded the MC. In the Birthday Honours List Sergeant White of 76 Audley Street was awarded the BEM. For his work with the Post Office, Mr Leonard Brown received the Imperial Service Medal, and for her work with the National Fire Service Mrs Violet Moore was awarded the MBE. For her work in Bomber Command operations, Leading Aircraftswoman J. Newman of 3 Kearsley Road was mentioned in despatches as was Leading Aircraftswoman J. Jenkins of 35 Wilderness Road for her work with Coastal Command.

Another Reading woman was mentioned in despatches after the war. Sister H. Mortimer of Coppice House, Loddon Bridge Road, was recognised for her gallant and distinguished service in Italy. Before the war she was a health visitor.

Leading Aircraftwoman J. Jenkins of 35 Wilderness Road was mentioned in despatches for her work with Coastal Command. She had been educated at Kendrick Girls' School.

The last evacuees left on 22 June when 212 children and 20 parents boarded a train to return to their London homes, leaving behind 900 evacuees who either had no home to return to or had decided to make their home in Reading. Two of those who chose to remain had arrived in September 1939 aged 10 and 12. By summer 1945 they had finished school and were working. They had enjoyed living with their wartime family so much they were not returning to their father in Mortlake. Mr and Mrs Clements of Piggotts Road, whose son had been killed in France in 1940, were delighted they were staying.

Summer meant holidays and some companies closed for a full week to give staff a break. As there were school children to amuse, a council sub-committee made arrangements for activities throughout August. The Corporation Swimming Baths were free on certain days at set times. There was a daily Punch and Judy show at 3pm in all the parks and recreation grounds, cricket and netball pitches were free to use, and sandpits were provided. For the first week of August there were morning and afternoon fishing competitions at Caversham Promenade with money prizes and on 4 August there was a sports day. Other events were added: folk dancing classes, a swimming gala in the Thames, model plane flying and a cycle polo match.

Again some families chose to spend their holiday helping the nation. Across Berkshire there were five harvest holiday camps where volunteers slept, five in a tent. A dining hut and recreational facilities were provided. They paid for their board/residence but the food provided was generous: breakfast – tea, fried bread, scrambled egg, bread, butter, jam; lunch – sandwiches, cake and tea; evening meal – soup, roast beef, Yorkshire pudding, two vegetables, cake and coffee. Manual labour in the camp was done by Italian PoWs although Italy had been fighting with the Allies for the last two years.

Once again a baby's parents were missing. On 17 July, a child between 18 months and 2 years-of-age was left with a couple until the weekend. When they did not return the couple went to the police who tried contacting the parents. A month later, George and Gillian White of 49 Testerton Street, London, were

In July 1945, another abandoned baby was investigated by the police. A month later the parents were traced to an address in London; they were charged with wilfully neglecting and abandoning their baby in a manner likely to cause it suffering.

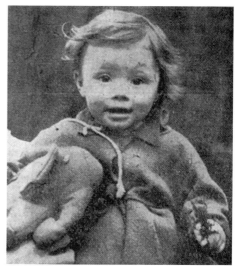

Another baby who was dumped in the town. This one was left in a public house.

charged with wilfully neglecting and abandoning their baby in a manner likely to cause it unnecessary suffering.

With the dropping of two atomic bombs, the war was over. One lady recalled what the end of the war had meant to her. 'My happiest memory was of my two brothers returning home at the end of the war. One had been in the army, the other in the navy. My mother wept tears of joy.'

Immediately after the announcement by the Prime Minister at midnight, celebrations began. 'Flags appeared, bonfires were lighted, fireworks soared into the skies, and train whistles and hooters broke the stillness of the night... the celebrations were quieter than on VE-Day. There were fewer decorations and illuminations at private houses, and although most of the churches held special services of thanksgiving, reports received indicate[d] that the attendances were not so large as on the previous celebration.'

Unfortunately the end of the war did not put an end to the Roll of Honour which listed thirteen Royal Berkshire Regiment dead; none were local. However, Lieutenant W. Vittle, RNVR, was reported dead after being missing since December 1944, as

A celebration in London Street to mark the end of the Second World War.

was Corporal D. Atkinson of 28 Coniston Drive who had been missing since February 1944. More Reading men arrived home after being released from Japanese PoW camps.

For many weeks after the end of the war in the Far East, PoWs from Japanese camps arrived in India and Sri Lanka.

Gunner Arthur Rumble, died on 30 August, aged 30. He was still a PoW even though the war had finished.

It was many more weeks before they were all home.

At the end of September, there was still a Roll of Honour for those killed in the Far East, and although it was peacetime, there were deaths among the occupying forces. Lance Corporal Peter Gray, of 47 Lamerton Road, was killed in an accident in Germany. He was an only son.

In September there were two fatal road accidents, both children under 15, 13 serious injuries and 22 slight injuries; a year earlier it had been 1 death, 11 seriously injured and eight slightly injured. It was a national problem RoSPA was trying to reduce.

Thanksgiving week began on 7 October with a service in Forbury

Gardens preceded by the ringing of church bells. Massed choirs performed excerpts from *The Messiah* in the Town Hall with dancing the next day. One highlight was a D-Day landing craft on the Thames giving trips in exchange for buying Savings Stamps. For those who did not want to brave the water, a Bailey bridge was erected over the Kennet and a Mosquito plane was on view at Thames-side Promenade. On the opening day there were tanks and guns in the Forbury. Naturally there was a sting

In November there was a thanksgiving parade in which service personnel and workers took part. At the top is the American army contingent and below women workers from Huntley, Bourne & Stevens.

These are Churchill tanks, one of the most produced British tank designs during the Second World War, with over 5,600 being built.

in the tail: the Mayor wanted townspeople to raise £1,000,000 in National Savings. By 19 October, the town, for the first time since 1940, failed to reach its target; it was £139,864 short.

In mid-October, Tutty's in London Street reminded everyone it was the first peace-time Christmas since 1938 (who needed reminding?) and that their Christmas toy fair was now open. The papers reported a surge in house building, with Cressingham Road being showcased. Just days later the first Pre-Fab arrived: it was erected on Whitley Wood Road over a month late. The delay was caused by labour shortages. Other sites were being prepared in Emmer Green, Oliver Dean's field and, using German PoW labour, the foundations were being laid at the Barnsdale Road – Windermere Road site.

The Standard was still reporting war deaths: Petty Officer Lewis Turner had died in a Japanese PoW camp on 5 September, twenty days after the war had ended. He was not the only one. Also reported as dying in Japanese hands were Aircraftsman First Class Bartlett and Leading Aircraftsman Bluck, both of Earley, and Sergeants Ednay and Tugwell.

Mrs Thompson of 53 Belmont Road received news that her husband, who had been a Japanese PoW since 1942, was safe.

Sidney Quick's death occurred in October 1944, but was not reported for well over a year. He was a Bevin boy who had died trying to rescue a colleague trapped down a coal mine.

The released PoWs in Reading jail were replaced by high profile detainees. The first was Private John Galaher who was accused of treason – a capital offence. It was alleged that after being captured at Dieppe in 1942, he acted as an informer for the Germans. The case was shrouded in secrecy and the authorities denied the existence of a further three men in the prison facing similar charges. Galaher received penal servitude for life, and two other prisoners, Hale and Martin, received 10 and 25 years imprisonment respectively. In May, 370 Canadian prisoners were sent to the prison after riots at Headley Detention Barracks in Hampshire. The last and most infamous prisoner, SS General Kurt Meyer, did not arrive until January 1946 and was only held for two weeks pending transfer to Canada.

Once again the troops received a welcome home but only the 1st Battalion received it and then it was only for 350 officers and men plus a detachment from 2nd Battalion. *The Standard* noted

After the war there were many people to reward for their bravery or service. Flight Lieutenant Ken Butterfield of Bath Road attended his DFC investiture with his aunt, a commandant in the Red Cross (left), and wife.

that 'the enthusiasm of the V-E and V-J Day crowds paled beside the unbounded vigour of the vast multitude that thronged the streets to welcome the battalion home. It was estimated that in the station and the immediate vicinity alone there were more than 10,000 people, and, in addition, Oxford Road was lined all the way to Brock Barracks by a wildly-cheering crowd who stood, in parts, five and six deep.'

On 4 November there was a parade of service personnel. Members of the Berkshire group of the ATS, attached to different branches of the army, took part in a Thanksgiving Service and Victory Parade. They marched through the town headed by the band of the REME.

Armistice Day fell on a Sunday, and by order of His Majesty the Two Minute Silence was universally observed at 11.00 am. The churches were full. An official ceremony was held for the first time since the start of the war, with the Mayor and Corporation attending a Service of Remembrance in the Forbury to which the public were invited. The two minutes silence was signalled by the firing of a maroon flare and concluded in the same way.

It was Christmas again. The war was over and demobilisation was proceeding slowly. It did not mean a return to the old days. Rationing continued, and the prospect of no oranges or bananas must have come as a disappointment, but there was the chance of grapefruit arriving. It was not U-boats stopping the ships but heavy gales.

What to do when you left the forces? Huntley & Palmers had the answer: work for them.

Neither did peace mean an end to recycling. The Wastepaper Recovery Association had a Christmas message: they wanted every family to save an extra half pound of paper instead of consigning the Christmas wrapping paper to the bin. It was estimated that this would provide 40 million sugar bags and 12 million square feet of plaster board, enough to make ceiling linings for 12,000 houses.

But Christmas 1945 was not as austere as expected. Additional rations, augmented by seasonal fare, put more food on the plate, and, according to *The Chronicle,* goodwill prevailed

What else could you put on a Christmas card in December 1945?

everywhere. The relaxation of austerity provided children with a pillowcase of presents and food instead of the usual stocking.

Four days before Christmas, the death of another PoW in Japanese hands was reported. It was confirmed that Lance Bombardier Pigg had died towards the end of 1942.

For many months into the New Year, news was received of the presumed deaths of men previously listed as missing. There were also accidental deaths among those waiting for demobilisation, those stationed abroad and those conscripted to work in the mines. The dying continued.

The British Army was scattered across the globe helping maintain peace. Private Grover was serving in Greece with 2 (Airborne) Battalion of the Ox & Bucks Light Infantry when he was killed in an accident on 5 February 1946.

The Second World War was over, but not for some parents. Many were trying to find out what had happened to their sons. Mr and Mrs J. Clargo of 13 Beresford Road were asking for information just before Christmas 1945. Their son Ernest is commemorated on the Singapore War Memorial. He had died on 5 March 1943.

All would gladly say farewell to 1945 in the hope that 1946 would be better. The Town Hall New Year's ball was more than a dance, it was also a party to celebrate the end of the greatest war the world had ever known.

Reading area locations bombed 1940-44

Area	Streets	Date
Caversham	Anglefield Road; Chiltern Road; Lower Henley Road; Oratory School; Pembroke Place; Star Road; Upper Henley Road	1 October 1940
	Kidmore End Road; Peppard Road	9 October 1940
	Buckside; Chester Street; Church Street; Hemdean Road; House Close; Meadow Road; Newlands Avenue; Oratory School; Oxford Street; Peppard Road; South Street	26 November 1940
	Church Road; Church Street; Clifton Park Road; Cromwell Road; Hemdean Road; Hemdean Rise; Henley Road; Lower Henley Road; North Street; Priory Avenue; Prospect Street; Rectory Road; Short Street; South View Avenue; St Anne's Road; St Peter's Avenue; St Peter's Church; Star Road; Westfield Road	30 January 1941
	Albert Road; Hemdean Road	10 February 1943
Coley	Berkeley Avenue; Castle Crescent; Dover Street; St Saviours Road; Wolseley Street	3 October 1940
	Coley Park Farm	15 November 1940
	Boston Avenue; Castle Crescent; Castle Lodge; Coley Avenue; Coley Recreational Ground; Ministry of Health	9 April 1941
Earley	Erleigh Court Gardens; Suttons Trial grounds	30 September 1940
	Bulmershe Woods	12 October 1940
	Suttons Trial Grounds	10 May 1941
	Beech Lane; Elm Road	19 June 1944 (flying bomb)

Reading	Brunswick Street	9 April 1940
	King's Road Gasworks	12 September 1940
	Cardiff Road; Salisbury Road	26 November 1940
	Baker Street; Bartletts Place; Basingstoke Road; Littlecote Drive; Mansfield Road; Tilehurst Road	9 April 1941
	King's Road Gasworks	10 May 1941
	King's Road Gasworks	12 May 1941
	Broad Street; Friar Street; Minster Street; St Laurence Church; Stone Street; Town Hall	10 February 1943
Tilehurst	Langley Hill	5 November 1940
	Westwood Row	19 November 1940
	Oxford Road	10 February 1943
Woodley	Woodley Airfield	16 August 1940
	South Lake	12 September 1940
	Woodley Airfield	16 September 1940
	Woodley Airfield	3 October 1940
	Butts Hill Road	30 January 1941
	Crockhamwell Lane; Ford Lane; North Lake	22 June 1942

Table based on Appendix 7 of *Early Closing Day*, M. Cooper, 2016.

Cooper estimates that 32 buildings were damaged/severely damaged with 41 fatal casualties, 51 serious injuries and a further 100 injured, caused by 113 bombs containing over 4½ tons of explosive. Bombs were also dropped on Arborfield, Shinfield, Theale, Three Mile Cross and Winnersh in 1940 and a V2 missile exploded over Cockpole Green in March 1945. Others were reported in the papers but not identified.

Bibliography

Andscomb, S., *Tilehurst*. Alan Sutton Publishing, 1995.

Burton, K.G. MA, *A Reception Town in War and Peace*. Planning Outlook, Vol. III, No. 3. Reprint. N.D.

Clapson, M., *Working-Class Suburb. Social change on an English council estate, 1930-2010*. Manchester UP, 2012.

Cooper, M., *Early Closing Day*. Scallop shell Press, 2016.

Corley, T.A.B., *Huntley & Palmers of Reading 1822-1972*. Hutchinson, 1972.

Crisp, D., *The History of Christ Church CE Primary School Reading 1868-2000*. Privately published, 2000.

Downs, D., et al, *Wilson School 100 Years of memories*. Corridor Press, 2006.

Earley Local History Group, *Earley Days*. Privately published, 2000.

Earley Local History Group, *Earley Memories*. Privately published, 2004.

Earley Local History Group, *Suttons Seeds, A History 1806-2006*. Privately published, 2006.

Hylton, S., *Reading at War*. Alan Sutton Publishing, 1996.

Hylton, S., *A History of Reading*. Phillimore, 2007.

Jeater, A., *The British Red Cross in Berkshire 1907 to 2007*. Privately published, 2007.

Nutbrown, G., *A Thames Parish Magazine Volume One 1869-1945*. Privately Published, 2015.

Philips, D., *The Story of Reading*. Countryside Books, 1999.

Railton, M. and Barr, M., *Battle Workhouse and Hospital 1867-2005*. Berkshire Medical Heritage Centre, 2005.

Railton, M. and Barr, M., *The Royal Berkshire Hospital 1839-1989*. Privately published, 1989.

Ramsey, W. (Ed.), *The Blitz Then and Now*. Battle of Britain Prints International, 1987-90.

Rooke, P., *Redlands, A hundred years at school*. Redlands School Parent Teachers' Association, 1991.

Sandall, A.G., *Are you 17?* Alan Sandall of Frome, 1993.

Southerton, P., *The story of a prison*. Osprey, 1975.

Stokes, A., *Pit of Shame. The Real Ballad of Reading Gaol*. Waterside Press, 2007.

Temple, J.C., *Wings over Woodley, The Story of Miles Aircraft and the Adwest Group*. Aston Publications, 1987.

The History of Tilehurst Group, *More Tilehurst memories*. 2007.

Watts, E., Platts, H., and Cobbold, J., *Copybooks to Computers. A celebration of 150 years of Earley St Peter's C of E (Aided) School 1848-1998*. Privately published, 1998.

Wheway, M.K., *The History of Ridgeway Primary School formerly Shinfield Road Council School 1929-2002*. Privately published, 2002.

Index